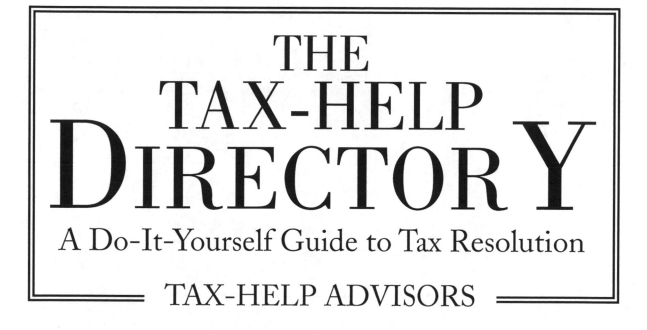

THE
TAX-HELP
DIRECTORY

A Do-It-Yourself Guide to Tax Resolution

TAX-HELP ADVISORS

abbott press®

A DIVISION OF WRITER'S DIGEST

Abbott Press books may be ordered through booksellers or by contacting:

Abbott Press
1663 Liberty Drive
Bloomington, IN 47403
www.abbottpress.com
Phone: 1-866-697-5310

Because of the dynamic nature of the Internet, any web addresses or links contained in this book may have changed since publication and may no longer be valid. The views expressed in this work are solely those of the author and do not necessarily reflect the views of the publisher, and the publisher hereby disclaims any responsibility for them.

Any people depicted in stock imagery provided by Thinkstock are models, and such images are being used for illustrative purposes only.
Certain stock imagery © Thinkstock.

ISBN: 978-1-4582-1678-6 (sc)
ISBN: 978-1-4582-1679-3 (e)

Library of Congress Control Number: 2014910814

Printed in the United States of America.

Abbott Press rev. date: 06/25/2014

CONTENTS

YOUR GUIDE TO THE GUIDE

WHAT IS A TAX-HELP DIRECTORY?

A Tax-Help Directory will provide you with a clear and concise method on how to *"Get the Tax problem Off Your Back!"* In a more simple way of stating, this guide will provide you the necessary information about the tax resolution concepts and philosophy which when properly executed, will provide you with the best possible outcome surrounding your particular tax issue.

THIS GUIDE **WILL** **NOT** HELP YOU...

- Prepare your income taxes
- Navigate the IRS directory of offices and phone numbers
- Bypass the IRS collection manual or other IRS guides and forms
- Get legal advice surrounding your tax matter

The Internet will provide you with more confusion, than help you. However, you can build your library with valuable information that will save you from thousands of dollars of interest and penalties that the IRS and State will impose on you.

The Tax-Help Directory is intended to cut through the hours of necessary research and sales pitches to give you exactly what you need to solve your tax problem, on your own. If you really desire to get the problem off your back, then read this book and follow the simple rules on how to eliminate your tax debt.

Any time you get lost or feel you need assistance, tax problem professionals are available to you via our website or toll free number.

THIS GUIDE <u>WILL</u> HELP YOU...

- Fill out IRS forms in a way that gives you more control over the results

- Learn how to keep the IRS from taking collection actions against you

- Fit your situation to Offer in Compromise parameters in order to qualify

- Trim your corporate payroll liability so the IRS can't shut you down

- Learn how to make the IRS and other agencies work your case for you

- Prepare a believable situation that the IRS must accept in order to manage a payment plan on your terms

- Plan your steps when the IRS says "no"

- Understand how to take control of your case when you receive a levy or garnishment

- Communicate better with the IRS and understand how to handle each conversation you have with IRS employees

- Take responsibility in order to ensure your matter gets done

IS THIS LEGAL?

This guide advocates full compliance and cooperation with the IRS. The federal government requires that we file and pay our taxes. They further require that we avoid tax schemes; non-compliance can result in unwanted legal persecution. The purpose of this book is to get you through the IRS system with the least amount of hassle while saving you time and money. All methods discussed in this guide adhere to IRS guidelines.

YOUR TAX-HELP DIRECTORY

The information in this guide does not constitute legal advice. Rather, it is a collection of information and instructions for how to navigate the complex procedural requirements imposed by the IRS. This guide is not intended to be all-inclusive with respect the IRS and any topics covered are always subject to change by the IRS. Make sure you do your own homework. The professionals at Tax-Help Advisors™ are in the business of providing advice and services only after an agreement is executed with an outline of services and fees. Call us to discuss your problem any time.

IF YOU STILL NEED HELP

Once you become familiar with this book, if you want to discuss what you have done with your situation, please call us. We will review, on the phone with you, your "plan of attack," and we will tell you whether it seems reasonable.

Do not gamble your hard earned money by representing yourself before the IRS. Get professional help now! Call (800) 838-6665, or email info@tax-help.com for answers.

THE DO'S AND DON'TS OF REPRESENTING YOURSELF

THIS IS YOUR REFERENCE GUIDE

Remember, this is not an all-inclusive book on the IRS. There are many pertinent legal issues, definitions, and rules when dealing with the IRS. For those of you who want to know various laws, codes, and so forth, purchase a book designed to teach you that. The purpose of this information is to show you our success in dealing with the IRS.

You can use our experience to outline the steps you will take to solve your IRS issues. If you need additional help, of any type, for a reasonable fee you can obtain a one-time phone consultation with Tax-Help Advisors™ to discuss you situation, and we can explain your options for how to resolve your issue.

If you need us to represent you before the IRS, please call or email us, and we will discuss what we can do for you. You can choose to do any of the following:

1. Represent yourself using the information in this book

2. Use the information in this book to keep tabs on someone you hired to represent you

3. Hire Tax-Help Advisors to represent you (safest alternative)

YOU CAN SETTLE

First, there are some basics you need to know. The IRS is not like any other company. Many experts see the IRS as an unsupervised group that makes up rules as it goes along. IRS personnel tend to do and say most anything to get you to do what they want. This is why many accountants find it very difficult to accomplish much when dealing directly with the collection personnel of the IRS. So how can you be successful?

The information we provide in this document is based on our dealings with the IRS over many years and shares the secrets we have learned to teach you how to settle with the IRS successfully.

ATTITUDE AND THE IRS PERSONNEL

Never ever complain to an IRS employee. They do not want to hear how sick you are, how poor you are, how bad the government is, how your ex-spouse or partner ripped you off, how good you were to pay most of the original principal portion of the taxes, or how your house flooded.

Some of that information is certainly essential for certain parts of the case, but don't whine or dump your troubles on the collection person. Stick with the facts. There will be a time and place to list your income, expenses, and reasons for certain things that happened.

POSITIVE RAPPORT

Being a collection person for the IRS can be a very difficult job. You can increase your chances that the situation will go favorably for you by being as accommodating as possible. Make the IRS person feel good and happy to be working with you (regardless of the person's response). What if you were asked to recite your full address, and then two minutes later were asked "What is your complete address?" How willing would you be to give your address the second time (instead of responding angrily by saying you already provided that information)? What about the third time? This kind of situation requires unlimited patience.

There is a difference between fighting with the IRS and sticking up for your rights. However, you may experience success if you are willing to let issues regarding your rights slide, concerning yourself with what matters most.

THE IRS ARE NOT OUT TO GET YOU

The IRS does not want to put you in jail. One must willfully perform a criminal act to be put in jail, and willful non-filing of an IRS tax return is a criminal act. However, the burden of proof is on the IRS to prove willfulness.

You must rid yourself of any fear or guilt concerning wrongdoing. When you contact the IRS, you will deal with the situation as it is today only. In 99% of collection cases, the only real questions are the following:

1. Where are your tax returns?
2. Will you "show me the money"?

The collection division wants any unfiled returns and wants to be satisfied concerning how taxes will be paid. During the discussion, you can deal with other issues, but not in place of these two.

Even if you stall the collection officer (as some advisors incorrectly advise), the manager may discover that the officer is not handling the responsibilities properly and issue a bank levy.

When you protest that you were waiting for the collection officer to look up a payment and get back to you, you will be told something like, "You had two months to provide him with the financial statement information and you didn't, so we levied your account." So much for stalling the collection officer. You have to take responsibility yourself to ensure that the case goes smoothly and quickly so no collection action is taken.

Rather than wasting your time on discussions about what the IRS can and can't do, accept that the IRS will do whatever it wants to do against you to collect delinquent returns and taxes. You can fare better by speaking up and defending yourself. Focus on simply taking care of business and leaving the history lessons, and the general IRS discussions, to the books you can buy off the shelf.

Maybe you want more time to file returns, more time to submit documents, a lower dollar monthly payment on a payment plan, or more favorable Offer in Compromise terms. Do not assume the IRS is out to get you or complain that they are being unfair.

You can expect to be burdened with short deadlines; two- to three-week deadlines may be issued when talking to Automated Collections (Automated Collections System). If they won't give you a longer period, you can hang up the phone and call back. Chances are that the log of the previous call will not be available yet, so the new person won't know you called minutes ago. Either way, you can accept the shorter deadline; then on the last day, call and explain that you are almost finished.

Tell them that you are willing to send the information in now by fax, and then overnight express, and ask if you can have a couple of days more to complete the information requested. Chances are that you will get the extension. If you have a revenue officer on your case, the IRS may well be a bit more liberal in granting you time.

THE RULES

Each collection or audit group operates independently in terms of how it does things. The rules can be different, they can change, or the person you are talking to may decide to "browbeat" you and not tell you the rules you are to follow. He or she may not even admit what the rules are or what rights you have even after you say that you know what the rules are.

Take the best you can get, and move on. You will see later that you have options along the way to sway things back in your favor. Usually you will have to decide whether the action is worth the time. Often it is not.

It is usually easier to bend to the IRS's timetable for tax preparation and the submission of documents. Of course, paying additional taxes is another matter. If the dollar amount is high, you will want to put the time and effort into saving the money.

BAD ASSUMPTIONS

You should provide the requested information as if you are talking to a computer that sometimes produces output that doesn't make sense. It is foolish to try to prove the computer is wrong. You must enter the IRS's world by its rules.

That's it for the general disposition you must have when dealing with the IRS. Following are a couple of things to be aware of.

IRS WEBSITE

The IRS website address is www.IRS.gov. This website will provide you with many links to all services provided by the IRS. Additionally, forms and instructions surrounding all programs sponsored by the IRS can be found here as well.

You can look up codes, revenue rulings, and even copies of the IRS manuals, including the collection manual. It's important to check dates because the website is not always kept up to date. Though this site is very comprehensive, it is typically not popular due to the difficulty in navigating specific areas.

The site is just a great source for forms and general information on areas you need learn more about. Also, sign up on the www.eftps.gov site for your personal and business payments.

At some point, you will need to make a payment quickly, and this will be the best way to do it. The payment posts the next day, and you get a tracking number to prove the payment was made; you won't have to rely on the bank or delivery service. It takes several weeks to get set up this service, so you must do so now, in anticipation of using it. It's free and worth the trouble.

THE IRS SERVICE CENTER

This department processes returns and sends out notices or errors, audits, and so on. You may get a letter showing a balance due, or various audit letters. If a letter shows a balance due then the first notice of "request for payment" is sent.

Other requests may be sent before the IRS sends the cp501 through cp504 series of notices. The cp504 is the notice of intent to levy. If not paid or resolved in 30 days, the account will be transferred to *Automated Collections System* division (ACS). *Automated Collections System* will issue a letter 1058, which is the final notice giving the taxpayer 30 days to appeal.

Of course, the IRS can skip this step and send it directly to a revenue officer (RO), who may levy your account before contacting you. So never let a notice of intent to levy go beyond the 30 days. Yes, the RO is supposed to issue a letter 1058, but he or she may do so simultaneously with the levy.

You decide if you want to handle it at *Automated Collections System* before it goes to a *Revenue Officer*. You need to take control and not be a victim.

TAX COURT

It is rare to have to resort to using tax court for a collection matter (or even an audit matter). Often, petitions to the tax court occur with the intention of getting the case transferred to Appeals. You can do this, too, by convincing the IRS that it will lighten their caseload.

Tell them that the tax court is full of unnecessary and frivolous cases and that yours is really an appeals case. The only reason you filed a court petition is that the time to file an appeal expired, so this was your only remedy.

THE TAXPAYER ADVOCATE

The taxpayer advocate is the group to approach when all else fails. Technically, this is an independent organization working in connection to the IRS and the taxpayer, however you will find the Advocate offices located within the very same halls of IRS regional offices. When trying to resolve a disagreement with an IRS employee, request to speak to the manager. If that fails and you still think the person is being unreasonable, you can go to the supervisor above or to the taxpayer advocate's office.

Should you call the Automated Collections System and are not getting anywhere with the Automated Collections System employee. Ask to speak to an Automated Collections System manager. This usually does not work that well, but a necessary step nonetheless.

Very often manager won't call you back so it is advisable for you to just continue to barrage the call center until you get someone who will provide you with reasonable service. There are hundreds of operators nationwide, so the chance that you would get the same operator more than once is improbable.

MANAGING YOUR CONVERSATION

Once you have reached an agent at a manager level, you will need to explain once again your issue and why you are calling. Get used to explaining you story over and over again. On this call, you will first need to verify the status of your case. It is important that you find answers to the following questions:

- Is your case is an Automated Collections System (ACS)?
- Is your case in the "Queue"?
- Has your case been transferred to a revenue officer?

If your case is in fact an Automated Collections System case, then Automated Collections System has control over it. If your case is waiting to be transferred to a revenue officer, the Automated Collections System employee can't really take action on it, so don't waste your time.

Always remember that any agent you speak with will be required to ask you questions and request that you provide updated information. While you never should be dishonest, it is always recommended that you avoid providing information prior to first consulting an advisor on the release of your information.

Always remember to stay in control of this call and when you have received the information you seek then simply hang up.

IF A REVENUE OFFICER CALLS

If you receive a phone call from your revenue officer, make sure you take the call or call back immediately. Revenue officers have a habit of levying accounts quicker than you think. Don't give them bank or work information, even if they press for it. Just tell them you need about two weeks to get everything together.

They will want to set up a meeting. Set it up for two weeks from now, preferably in their office, if they will allow it. Another benefit of having a representative is that the meetings are mostly in the representative's office, so the IRS doesn't poke around your home or business.

Spend the time leading up to the meeting getting your financial statements and backup information together. Look up the IRS table expense allowances for the expenses on the 433A, and put together a picture of your income and expense information and asset situation.

Know ahead of time what assets the IRS will allow you to keep and the likelihood of them allowing each expense deduction. You have a greater chance of getting what you want if you are prepared.

If you are dealing with a revenue officer (henceforth RO), do not let him or her browbeat you into submission. You have the right to hire a representative and have time before disclosing your financial information to them. ROs will try to get you to answer questions about marital status, business identification numbers, and so forth. Even if you think the answers are easy and won't hurt you, don't give them. You are establishing a rapport that allows the RO influence over you for future questions if you do so.

In addition, you may give information you will want to retract later. Just keep insisting that you are you, give the RO your social security number, and verify your address; say that for the rest, you will get back to him or her on the date of the meeting.

If the RO doesn't want to wait two weeks, you can agree to a meeting in one week with an agreement from the RO to an extension if necessary. If the RO requests that you meet sooner, ask for the manager's name and phone number (which you should do anyway, from the start) so that you can find out why you can't have two weeks. The RO may change the date or try to browbeat you into not calling. Say that you are not calling to complain about the RO. This is very important and should always be said when you ask for someone's manager.

Never get mad and say, "Give me your manager!" The RO will take that as a threat and can get very tough. Just say you want the manager's opinion about the appointment date because you think it is unreasonable. Don't be surprised if the manager gives you more time. However, the manager may also try to intimidate you for calling. No problem; this way you find out early on whether you have a good manager or one who doesn't police the revenue officers in his or her group. This information will help you make decisions later.

If you are really getting frustrated dealing with the collection division and they are about to issue a lien, or levy, or take other collection action, you could call the taxpayer advocate group. You can look up www.irs.gov/advocate or just Google "Taxpayer Advocate" for the Form 911.

It's easy to fill out, but when they get busy, they will attempt to make little of your hardship reason. Be careful to explain, and attach an additional sheet if necessary, that you will suffer great hardship if they don't intervene.

Explain exactly what you want them to do. If you have to get them involved because the RO has threatened to take enforcement action due to a short deadline or some other petty reason, then so be it. File your 911 by fax and call the advocate group's office to follow it up.

Another reason the advocate group uses to turn down a case is lack of proof that the current action is a burden to you. You can't assume that collection action will take place. You actually have to ask the RO what will be done if you miss your one-week deadline (for example).

The RO may say nothing will be done or that they will likely just issue a letter. Until you know what's in that letter, you may not have the level of hardship required for an advocate case. The letter may just be a second request (a formal one) for documents. So make sure you can explain, in detail, the exact action that is imminent and will cause you the hardship you foresee happening to you.

The taxpayer advocate works with the IRS, often in the same building. You should call them to see if they will take your case. Use them for help when dealing with the collection division or the Offer in Compromise division, not the audit division.

One good thing about the taxpayer advocate's office is that it has greater ability to get the attention of the collection division. It is taken very seriously, and the collection division will respond promptly to the office.

DID YOU MOVE?

When you move, file a change of address form 8822 with the IRS. File it certified return receipt, and keep a copy of the form and proof of mailing. Many people don't give the IRS their address change as a way to put more distance between themselves and the IRS.

This is a big mistake. If you get notices on time, you can avoid collection action easier and have a better chance at stopping the liability or claim against you. Now that you know how to deal with the IRS, file form 8822 when you change your address.

TAX RETURN EXTENSIONS

If you can't complete and mail your 1040 personal tax return by April 15th, file an automatic extension form 4868. It's very easy to fill out. Read the instructions on the form, and remember that you don't have to pay the amount estimated.

You only have to put down approximately what the liability will be when you file the return. Don't try to lower the amount; in fact, estimate a bit high. A high estimate will aid you in avoiding late filing penalties.

If you can't pay at the time of filing, file on time and also file Form 1127, the application for extension of time to pay. (You must show reasonable cause.) The strict requirements are listed on the back of the form.

File this application for the situations described on the form. Download the form and become familiar with the acceptable reasons for granting it. You have nothing to lose by trying it on your own.

If you need more than six months to pay, you can avoid the collection officer by filing Form 9465 with your return. Form 9465 is an Installment Agreement request. If your liability is under $10,000, they must accept it as long as you meet the rules printed on the form.

You can also try it for balances greater than $10,000. If your request is accepted, you avoid dealing with the collection division.

Just be sure you don't show that you can pay more than the amount offered; if you have equity in your house or a retirement plan, they will want a larger payment or perhaps payment in full.

Only submit financials with form 9465 if you are "proud of how poor you are" and confident that you have nothing that they can touch.

UNFILED, DELINQUENT OR MISSING RETURNS

If you have back tax returns to file, the IRS can and will use the delinquent returns against you in many ways. For example, if you have a refund coming to you, and you file more than three years past the due date (including valid extensions) the IRS will keep the refund.

The IRS will not even offset the refund against a tax liability from another year. (However, computer errors have sometimes done this).

If you are in a "binding" Installment Agreement to pay a prior tax liability or are in an uncollectible status, the filing of any return or the paying of any tax late will void the agreement and cause all money to become due immediately.

Often when an agreement is in default, taxpayers find out via a levy on their bank account or paycheck. Even worse, taxpayers may find out through a levy on their spouse's paycheck or a lien on their house and other property.

Taxpayers are not always notified first. Sometimes, even the representative is not notified. The IRS may have filed a return for you, charged you with the tax, and is now about to take collection action against you; You may not even know it yet. You are about to find out the hard way.

Even if you like the way they prepared the returns, (probably because they charged you with less tax than you thought you owed), you still need to sign the return. Otherwise, the statute of limitations on assessment does not run.

This means that the IRS can audit you and/or charge you with additional taxes at any future time. Normally they have three years from the time you send a return in. Even if you are not required to file, you should file anyway. Doing so will protect you from having to prove that you were not required to file many years after the fact.

UNFILED (OR DELINQUENT) TAX RETURNS

You need to file any unfiled back tax returns immediately. Even if you are missing records, are afraid that there is a possibility of owing money, are confused about how to fill out the returns, or are afraid to tell the IRS where you are, you still need to file now. That is, assuming you owe more money than you can send in with the returns. Let's examine your choices.

You have no IRS problems other than that you have failed to file one or more years of back tax, or have delinquent returns. You received an IRS letter asking for the return. If you can pay the balance in full plus interest and penalties, then send the IRS the return with your check for the money owed. Write the check out to "U.S. Treasury" and send it with the returns to the office that requested it.

The problem comes when either you are contacted by a RO or Automated Collections System asking for money from returns the IRS filed for you or the IRS sends you a cp2000 or other letter proposing a liability. This could be based on a W2, 1099, K-1, and so forth sent to the IRS reporting income in your behalf. In such a case, you must take actions to refute the liability or make arrangements to establish an installment agreement or other method of payment.

BUSINESS PAYROLL TAX AND YOUR SANITY

TRUST FUND PENALTY, IRS CODE 6672, CIVIL PENALTY (THESE TITLES ALL REFER TO THE SAME THING)

Whenever a company owes payroll taxes (withholding, Social Security, and Medicare taken out of the employee's paycheck), the liability can extend to any and all responsible parties. When corporations or legal liability companies (not general partnerships or sole proprietorships) owe payroll, only the trust fund can be charged to a responsible party.

The trust fund can be significantly less than the total owed by the company. The trust fund consists of the federal withholding; Social Security (FICA), and Medicare tax that remains unpaid after the IRS takes into consideration the payments that are made and applied to each quarter. The remaining unpaid trust fund gets charged to each responsible party that the IRS feels owes the tax.

You owe the trust fund when you take part in the decision-making process for the company funds. Do you help decide who gets paid and who doesn't get paid? Do you sign the checks? The IRS would have you believe that you are liable for the trust fund if you are a signature authority on the company bank account, if you signed checks, if you are a stockholder, or if you signed tax reports.

The law, however, states that if you sign checks as a convenience for the employer, you do it only when you are told to do so, and you don't have any authority to decide who to pay or when and how much, proving this should get you out of the liability.

However, the IRS knows that anyone can say that, so you need further evidence, such as notarized statements from people you worked side by side with who can testify that they never saw you make such decisions. Professional help may be needed here. Testimony from the actual people liable (such as the owner) is good too. Your statements should never be in conflict with statements made by other potentially liable people.

Why is this significant? Because of the legal entity concept and other rules, the IRS can look only to the assets of the company for payment of the full debt. If the company doesn't have any assets or has minimal value (approx. $3,100 forced sale value), the IRS can collect only the remaining trust fund from the responsible parties.

If you are about to be assessed a trust fund from a company and you are not liable, you must attempt to prove this to the collection personnel as soon as possible. The IRS is required to fill out an IRS form 4180 interviews before determining who is liable. This is where they collect evidence to determine who is liable for the trust fund.

It is to your advantage to meet with the collection officer or discuss with Automated Collections System your position so you can sway that person to your way of believing. Just answer the questions as briefly as possible. Do not volunteer additional information.

Obtain a copy of form 4180 first from the Internet so you know what questions you will be answering and are not caught off guard. If you can't convince them that you don't owe the tax, you will have to prepare an appeal (see the Appeals chapter).

If you don't appeal this action and the trust fund is charged to you, it will be treated as a tax you owe under your social security number. There is little restriction as to what the IRS can levy or seize to collect this debt. The trust fund debt will be treated like a debt from your personal tax return Form 1040.

This debt will be forgiven as part of an Offer in Compromise or if the statute of limitation period on collections expires. (A bankruptcy won't get rid of the trust fund liability—not even a Chapter 7.) It is possible to have the trust fund removed from your Record of Account when the statute runs out.

Sometimes the IRS will not be upfront with you about this and tries to get you to pay after the statute runs out. Don't fall for it. The IRS is very good at convincing taxpayers to give up their rights and not believe their advisors. It will do you good to look up the rules yourself if you ever have doubts about the advice you are following. Anytime you want more technical information, you could buy a book or look up the IRS version on their website.

When you want to test the IRS's calculation of the actual trust fund owed, you need to request Form 4183 and check how the actual payments toward the trust fund were applied. Get copies of the Record of Account for each period they say you owe. Make sure you know when each payment was made and for how much.

Compare this to Form 4183 and make sure the payments were included and offset against the actual tax. In many cases, the IRS has filed a 6020B and did not accept the actual late return, thereby inflating the trust fund. There have also been errors in the trust fund calculation when late payments were treated as future payments and applied toward the non-trust fund, leaving a greater trust fund balance.

If you are one of the owners of the company, you should consider whether it is best to pay the taxes or to liquidate and just pay the trust fund.

OFFER IN COMPROMISE; THE HOLY GRAIL?

THE OFFER IN COMPROMISE

Despite what you may have been led to believe, you may, or may not qualify for an offer in compromise (OIC) depending on many important and components relating to your personal situation. Here is a basic breakdown of the variables as the IRS see's fit to determine your eligibility.

A two-part formula is used to determine whether you qualify. Take your income, and deduct allowable expenses (you need the IRS allowable expense chart for this). Your result is the amount the IRS feels you can pay each month after paying your "necessary living expenses." Then multiply this number by fifty. Next, add it to the equity (that is how much you pocket for yourself if you sell the item at a bargain sale) in each of your assets.

For example, add the equity in your house, car, retirement plan, rental property, stocks, and so forth to fifty times the monthly amount. Multipliers may vary; this is just an estimate. The result is the total amount the IRS expects from you now in a lump sum. Or if you can pay it out over two years (maybe more) with interest added instead. This calculation is subject to the IRS's opinion of the value of your assets and the allowances they will give you when computing how much money you have available to pay monthly.

The Offer divisions take the attitude that they are not obligated to do an Offer for anyone unless they want to. They also get pressured to meet quotas, and do so at the last minute. Thus, non-qualifying offers sometime get accepted, while qualifying ones (really deserving ones) sometimes do not.

Obviously you do not want your offer to be turned down. Offers need to be worked consistently (it is not a static process); it is not terribly uncommon for an Offer process to take over a year. The good news is that Offers can be quickly filed again after they are turned down.

Download the Offer in Compromise book from the IRS's website. The key to a low Offer is in the 433A and 433B (if needed). Please review chapter 10 concerning these forms. Offers are also used to resolve a doubt as to liability.

Say that you are charged a tax that you really don't owe and you have either exhausted your appeal rights or they have expired. Filing an offer is a way to get these rights back. You present your best argument to the offer division, and if you are of low income, even though the instructions say that a 433A is not necessary, fill one out anyway.

Doing so shows that your income is low, especially if the expense items allowed are less than your income. The IRS will probably be more sympathetic if they know they can't get more money out of you anyway.

YOUR CHECKLIST FOR FILING AN OIC

1. Prepare an Offer—download Form 433A (and 433B if needed) and Form 966. Use 656-A for your income certification if your income is low enough that you are exempt from paying the application fee and/or payments. Use form 656-PPV to accompany any monthly payments you make under the offer, starting with the first one. Mailing addresses will vary, so please check the one for the offer location you are sending to.

2. Fill out the forms, and send them along with your backup receipts, payment of processing fee, and required payment. See the instructions for computing this. Also check the chart to see whether you are exempt from paying the fee and/or payment.

3. Do follow-up calls and be sure that your Offer is accepted for processing.

4. Respond in a timely manner to requests for additional information. Make sure the offer division acknowledges receipt of the information prior to their deadline.

5. Make sure you have a conversation with the offer specialist prior to their preparation of what the offer amount should be. Call and ask how the review is going, and let them know you are available for questions. This way you can explain things before they come to conclusions on their own.

6. Don't argue too much; this is your big chance for a reduction. You will probably have to pay more than you think is fair. Just make sure they don't make big unfair adjustments against you. Don't sweat the small stuff.

7. If you think they are grossly wrong about what you should have to pay, you can appeal or submit an Offer later.

8. Exercise patience. Offers get kicked around a lot and may have to be re-filed in the process. Yes, you will have to update the forms and redo your proof of income and expenses. Maybe more than once. Hang in there, and remember to be patient. It hopefully will be worth it all in the end.

9. Be prepared, even a year later, to submit updated income and expense information. Make sure your income didn't go up and you didn't pay a large expenditure.

CRITICAL INFORMATION

If the IRS feels that your situation is temporary and it benefits them to do so, they may elect to average the prior three years. The burden of proof will be on you to show that your current immediate situation is an accurate projection of your income over the next five years (or remaining statute of limitations on collections).

You will have to show that the last-three-year average is higher than your projection because of an extraordinary situation that is not likely to repeat itself.

The Offer division likes to use the prior year's tax return as a guide for showing what your income and expenses are. If it is within the first few months of the year, and it benefits you to do so, then use that. Of course you will then have to lower your income over the next few months so that it closely resembles or is less than the prior year.

It is beneficial to look at income and expenses "per month" so that you can group together a number of previous months as a way to support what you are representing as your income and expenses on Form 433A.

For example, it is September and you are preparing your 433A to submit as part of an Offer in Compromise. You could include the info for July through September (three months, as the instructions show) or expand it to June through September, or March through September if that would be more favorable for you. Also, include information about projected future income. Give them proof beyond just your word.

Get letters from your physician to support that your current medical condition does not allow you to work more hours than you currently are working. This will support your claim of a low income, too. The more proof, the better.

If you own a house, get an appraisal of it that supports the value you claim. If it is close to their estimate, they will likely use your appraisal. If there is a very large difference, they will push for their value. In this issue, IRS Appeals will force the collection division to use what they feel is the most reasonable value.

Does your spouse stay home to care for your healthy teenage kids? The Offer division may not accept a spouse not working. You will be hard pressed to prove that it is absolutely necessary for your spouse to not work even part-time. Maybe the spouse should get a job before you file the Offer. Yes, it will hurt the Offer amount, but it will increase the chances of acceptance.

The main taxpayer, who has the liability (or joint liability), needs to be working, too. You should not file saying that you were laid off last month and that you are looking for a job. Get a job before you file. Remember, the IRS has to be comfortable that the Offer amount they accept is the most that they can get out of you over the remaining collection statute. Obviously, once you do get a job, your income will be higher, so your ability to pay them more money will be greater.

It's OK to file the Offer before you receive your first paycheck on your new job. Just indicate on your cover letter that you will send in the pay stubs when you receive them.

Sometimes the liability is just yours. However your spouse must take part in the Offer process and sign the financial statement (433A), including his or her income and expenses to arrive at the monthly amount available after allowable expenses are deducted from income, even though he or she may not be liable for the tax and will not be signing the Offer Form 966.

If you are married and have a prenuptial agreement or have kept your income, expenses, income tax filing, and so forth separate, you have a good argument for keeping your spouse's information out of the offer process.

You will be able to deduct only half of your living expenses, so you must determine which way benefits you the most. Usually if your spouse has an income much greater than his or her share of the living expenses, it is better to use half of the deductions and only your income. Different states follow different practices, so always be prepared to carefully explain and document what you are doing.

HOW TO "NOT" BREAK YOUR PAYMENT PLAN OR OIC

You do this by keeping in compliance. This means filing and paying on time as follows.

Each taxpayer is responsible for her own company and individual compliance with tax filings and payments of taxes as well as installments under an IRS agreement.

You cannot obtain an Installment Agreement or an Offer, or even appeal a decision (and get proper consideration) from an IRS employee, without all of your tax returns filed. All income tax returns and all business returns you are associated with must be filed.

INDIVIDUALS
(NONBUSINESS)

All installment payments must be received (and noted as such by the IRS) by the due date. The payment should clearly reflect what periods and years are being paid.

Even if taxes are being taken out of your paycheck and you never had to make payments before, if you owe tax when you file your return, you will break your installment agreement.

In fact, any liability assessed to your personal social security number will break the agreement. This includes trust fund from a corporation in which you were a responsible party for the corporation not paying their payroll taxes. It does little good to establish an agreement if you know that sometime in the near future you will have a tax liability assessed to you.

INDIVIDUALS
(WITH PAYROLL FROM A SCHEDULE C BUSINESS)

In addition to the above, all payroll deposits must be made on time for the correct amount. It is your responsibility to ensure that this happens. If you hire an accountant or payroll service, make sure you review the worksheets and verify that the amount is correct and that the payments are made on time.

Many Installment Agreements and Offers are broken because people trusted others to do just this. It's OK to hire someone to help, but be sure to take the extra step to ensure that it is being done right.

All tax reports (the ones applicable to you)—1120,1120s, 1065, 941, 940, 1120 ES, and so on must be filed on time. This means by the due date, including any extensions. Timeliness is critical. If mailing, check the correct address and send registered receipt.

OFFER QUALIFYING

Individuals must of course have their 1040 personal returns and current estimated taxes filed and paid on time. If you have payroll, you must have the last two quarters paid on time.

FORM 656 INSTRUCTIONS

SECTION I.

Remember that separate offers need to be submitted for each account. So pull the records of account under your social security number, your spouse's social security number, and the joint numbers. Make sure your returns are filed correctly. Sometimes the accounts are mixed up. Call Automated Collections System and have them fix the records of account. Once straightened out, or even before it is straightened out, especially if you have a collection deadline, prepare your Offer in Compromise forms.

Any liabilities for periods under a separate ID number must be put on a separate 656 as a separate offer with a separate offer fee.

A joint liability will require a separate joint offer form, too.

Any business liabilities under a separate ID number will be a separate offer as well. However, different business IDs can be combined on the same Offer form.

As seen above, depending on who the Offer is for, you will have up to three separate forms to fill out. You can divide your offer amount proportionally under each form. Put a note on the forms to alert the reviewer at the IRS which other offer forms are part of your offer request. They will consider all of them together.

SECTION II.

Fill in section 1 with the correct name, address, and ID number.

SECTION III.

Fill in the type of liabilities you are attempting to compromise. They will be the periods and years that show up on the Record of Account that you pull from the IRS. Your RO can obtain this for you, but you may prefer to submit your own request just in case they leave some periods of liabilities out. However, the worst that can happen here is that the Offer gets kicked back to you with a request to include the periods you left out. Then you make the adjustments and send it back to the Offer division.

SECTION IV.

If you are submitting an Offer based on doubt as to liability, meaning that you don't owe it in the first place, you must fill out Form 656-L instead of this form. The two choices are doubt as to liability and effective tax administration. The first one is the most common. That is why you are filing this Offer in the first place. You can't pay off the full amount within the statutory period of collection.

Just check this box if your assets can fully pay off the liability but your exceptional circumstances would cause an undue hardship. After the IRS cleans you out of your assets and the biggest monthly payment you can possibly make, who wouldn't suffer an "economic hardship?" But the IRS has a different interpretation than most.

For example, that you are 70 years old and your health is bad. You are living on Social Security, and you have equity in your house greater than your tax liability. You've lived there for 30 years and paid off the mortgage. Using the offer formula, your house is worth $200,000 (80% is $160,000), and you only owe $120,000. You don't qualify for an offer under doubt as to ability to pay.

But given your health and income situation, if you borrowed against the house, you couldn't make the payments. You probably wouldn't qualify for a loan anyway. Not to mention, moving you out of the house would cause great emotional stress. You should argue for a minimum offer because the IRS can't get more money from you.

They may argue that you take out a reverse mortgage and pay them whatever the bank is willing to give. If that occurs, you should hire a professional to take the situation from there. These are hard Offers to get accepted, and every tax professional has had trouble doing so.

SECTION V.

The terms: You will have to go back and forth with the IRS many times to be sure this section is straight. Be careful to read the instructions and do the math. Don't sweat this; if the offer specialist thinks the amounts should be different, he will send the Offer back and ask you to redo it. No problem; you already know he will probably do that anyway.

SECTION VI.

These are the conditions you are agreeing to, with the IRS boldly pointing out to you what they require of you. You give away some legal rights here. Sometimes it is easier to file an Offer based on doubt as to ability to pay than to go to Appeals to lower an audit adjustment.

For instance, suppose you are audited, and the adjustment causes you an additional tax liability of $100,000 on top of the $50,000 you already owe for that year. You could pay someone to fight an appeals case to lower the $150,000 to perhaps $120,000 (because you have receipts and you think the auditor was not fair).

However, you may feel that the trouble is unnecessary because you project that you will only have to pay $40,000 at most in an Offer, based on your calculations. Now you sign part V(j), which says, "Upon acceptance of the Offer you agree to give up your rights to contest the liability." You do the Offer and break it later because you missed a payment.

Too bad—you just lost the $30,000 potential adjustment (that reduced the liability from $150,000 to $120,000). You can avoid this by making sure you do everything possible to lower a tax liability before you file an Offer. Sometimes it's easier said than done. Please take the time to understand each section as thoroughly as possible.

SECTION VII.

Explanations of circumstances—representatives sometimes do not put in the time and attention needed here. You are painting a picture for the IRS to see how poor you are and that you lack the ability to pay the liability in full. So make sure you let them know of your illnesses, lack of education, lack of skills, and so on.

Tell them about the recent depression, downturn in business, current layoffs in your company, business contract that probably won't renew, alcohol program you just joined, psychologist you are going to, drugs for medical conditions you are taking, and so on. Make them realize how bad your life is in the first place, on top of now having to give them most everything you have to settle the liability.

You should not tell them that you would file a bankruptcy if they don't accept an Offer. They may take this as a threat and tell you that if you are going to file for bankruptcy, then you should do so.

SECTION VIII.

Source of funds: Usually just write that money will be borrowed from family and friends, if it is a lump sum offer. Don't give names or other identifiers unless they specifically ask.

SECTION IX.

If your financial statements do reveal that you have the cash available for a lump sum offer, then the Offer amount will be more, as the formula to compute the offer amount will show. Sign and date the Offer.

SECTION X.

If you are not able to communicate with the IRS and have a friend or family member helping you, fill this part out.

SECTION XI.

For your Power of Attorney representative.

SECTION XII.

As with the previous section, unless you use two different people. Maybe you have an accountant friend who was willing to fill out the forms but not willing to represent you, and a friend or family member who will speak to the IRS for you. This is a dangerous situation. The person speaking to the IRS should be knowledgeable about the financial information if at all possible.

THE NIGHTMARE ON LIEN
AND LEVY STREET

LIENS, LEVIES, AND SUBORDINATION

- **LIEN**

  A legal claim against real property filed in a county courthouse

- **LEVY**

  A levy is the action of taking an asset (wages, bank account, etc.) to satisfy payment of a debt

- **SUBORDINATION**

  Subordination entails permission from the IRS to allow another creditor a higher collateral security position in your assets

A good source for detailed information regarding lien subordination is IRS Pub 764. Search for it on your computer and download a copy for your review. It has a great section on how to prepare the application and what to do afterward.

REASONS THE IRS WILL GIVE YOU
A LIEN SUBORDINATION

1. You can offer approximately three times the value of your liability as collateral, or you can buy an insurance bond for approximately three times the liability.

2. You can show that it will be easier for the IRS to collect more money by doing the subordination (e.g., getting all the proceeds on the sale of your house).

The following points should be helpful for your success:

You should acknowledge that you could and probably should have stopped this much earlier in the collection process. Understand that the IRS is not going to be sympathetic to your concerns about how tough it will be to successfully conduct your business.

The IRS puts a lien on to protect itself against third-party creditors getting your assets before they do. So why would they be willing to give up their creditor protection? Their general policy is not to remove or subordinate liens (or levies) unless you fit one of their acceptable categories.

First consider the question of whether or not you can live with the lien. It's usually not as bad as you initially thought. Is it hurting your credit? By the way, the IRS does not file the lien with the credit bureaus; so don't ask the credit bureaus to take it off.

The credit bureaus pick up the lien on their own from courthouse records. You can remove it for a short time by sending a letter to the credit bureau explaining that this is not yours, (assuming that it isn't), or that it is grossly overstated.

If there is no confirming response within 30 days, the credit bureau must remove it until they receive a confirming response. But this is the subject for a manual on credit repair. In any case, you can use someone else's credit or refrain from using any credit till the liability is paid or resolved.

Many times the people you buy from will be sympathetic and help you work around it. You should consider living with the lien and focusing on paying off the liability as soon as possible. It is better than throwing your money away by paying some misleading representative who promises to remove the lien using some type of trick or exceptional experience.

Liens are specific to the county where they are filed. Nevertheless, it is better to sell the property and give that money to the IRS to lower your debt than to spend the time and money to untangle it once the lien is filed in that county.

You can also sell property that you have a lien on. What? Well, you can't convey title, but if you sell it for fair market value, you have not broken any laws. Who would buy it? A relative or friend or someone else who really wants the property and who understands and is willing to wait for the IRS to release the property once the fair market value (money) is offered to them. The risk here, of course, is that the IRS should agree with your value of the real estate. It is not recommended that you do this on your own.

On the other hand, if your asset is not real property, the IRS has greater trouble recovering the transferred property. Many people have sold their cars or boats and pulled the money from their bank accounts while a levy was in place and got away with it.

We can't advise anyone to do this without knowing all the details of their situation. Most people will be safe taking out cash, especially if that can show that it went to food, rent or mortgage, medical, and other general living expenses.

IF YOU NEED A LIEN SUBORDINATION

1. Liens really hurt companies when sales and financing are inhibited. A business could be ruined without subordination. Subordination may be needed so a bank or accounts receivable financing company may become a first-position creditor.

2. Make sure you answer all items on the application for a Certificate of Subordination of Federal Tax Lien, and include all documents that explain what you are trying to show them. Then when finished, sit back and ask yourself, "If I were an IRS employee and got my application, would I understand and approve it?"

   Would you be convinced that it was in the IRS's best interest to let you continue your business without the lien and pay them back the money you owe? If not, go back and make any necessary changes.

3. When you are satisfied, send it to your RO and call to make sure they received it. Find out when they plan on sending it to the subordination group of the IRS. Then call at that time to make sure it went out.

If you don't have an RO assigned to your case, simply contact the subordination group directly. Request that they handle it immediately if time is of the essence. Be polite, and remember to ask as if you're asking for a favor. Make the appropriate follow-up calls to get it through the system.

4. Bad News; the IRS gets a lot of these requests, so it still may take from two weeks to three months. Sometimes it is hard to convince the IRS that it is in their best interest to do the release. Federal government moves slowly, to its own disadvantage sometimes. Some companies have gone out of business because they could no longer factor their accounts receivable.

5. You could file an emergency collection appeal to release the lien, but it still has to go through the subordination group. The collection appeal could be used prior to the lien being filed or to appeal levies and other collection actions. Now you see why it is so important to head off a lien before it happens when you intend to sell real property to help pay off an IRS debt. Don't become a victim to this.

6. You can always take this to the Taxpayer Advocate's office. If you prove the hardship to them, they may take your case.

7. If you can show that the IRS didn't give proper notice, such as a notice of deficiency or another 30-day notice, you can appeal the lien. However, even if you win, you still didn't resolve the problem; they can always put it back on once they cure the notice issue.

   You don't fare better in Appeals one way or the other, so why not just do a CDP (collection due process) or CAP (collection appeals program) appeal based on hardship, establishing a payment plan, Offer in Compromise, and so on?

   During the time spent fighting a lien based on not being given proper notice, you would lose any buyer for your property that you may have attracted. The IRS publication 1660 explains your appeal rights. Obtain a copy from the IRS' website.

8. You can get a release to obtain a bank loan.

LIEN RELEASES

Call to discuss lien releases with the IRS at (800) 913-6050; this division specifically handles lien releases and should provide you with all you need to get this done.

Assuming you have paid the liability, or, should have been removed for another reason and you need to remove the lien. Once the liability is fully paid, the lien is no longer valid and you should have no problem getting it removed. If for some reason you encounter difficulty, contact the Taxpayer Advocate's office for help.

If you want a lien released because of hardship reasons and have been unsuccessful through the primary channels, you will need to file an appeal.

You should file an appeal directly with the collection officer or Automated Collections System. If no one is assigned, you can file directly with your local Appeals office. Be careful; sometimes Appeals secretaries say they can't accept an appeal unless it comes to them from collections, don't believe it.

If you are about to suffer a hardship and you have no one in collections assigned to your case, just call an Appeals officer or visit your local Appeals office and get them to accept your appeal.

THOSE LETTERS & NOTICES; WHAT DO THEY MEAN?

ABOUT IRS LETTERS AND NOTICES

You should always respond letters and notices if you want to protect your rights or initiate an action. The further into the collection process you wait to make a correction, the harder and more time consuming it will be. People have paid tax professionals thousands of dollars to correct actions that would have been very simple, and less costly, if done the moment the IRS first contacted them.

This section of the Tax-Help Directory will give you better information about how to respond to various notices. This section will provide you with a list of notices common to an outstanding tax balance and their brief descriptions. Should you receive a notice not found in this list pleas go to the IRS website or search via your computer search engine.

- **NOTICE OF A CHANGE TO YOUR RETURN**
  (FORM CP11)

  This notice reflects adjustments the IRS made to your return and the effect it had on penalties and interest. In addition, you will typically see an increase to your tax liability calculation. The longer you are in the collection process, the harder it will be to undo this action. To understand the reason for the changes, contact the IRS and ask. You don't have to answer questions beyond the verifying questions to prove that you are you, and you do not have to make promises of when you will make payments. Just say you will call back soon after looking into the matter.

- ## FINAL NOTICE OF INTENT TO LEVY
  (FORM CP11)

This is also a notice to you of your right to a hearing. You have 30 days to appeal. You should consider solving the case before that time and getting the *Revenue Officer* to hold off on the levy. Appeals are time consuming and still won't solve the compliance issues of filing delinquent returns or payment issues of paying delinquent taxes.

If you can't file the delinquent taxes and fill out the collection information statements within the 30 days, call the *Revenue Officer* to explain your desire to cooperate. Show your sincerity and willingness to cooperate and you will probably be granted additional time. If you are not granted additional time, simply call back to discuss with a different agent.

- ## REQUEST FOR TAX PAYMENT
  (FORM CP14)

This is your first bill for taxes due. The IRS feels that you still did not pay enough to cover the liability plus interest and penalties. This letter will go to great lengths to explain the interest and penalties, and often less about why you owe money.

- ## CHANGES MADE AS RESULT OF AUDIT
  (FORM CP22E)

This is a change based on the result of an IRS audit. You don't even have to be aware of having been through an audit. The IRS can and does conduct audits without your knowledge.

If they think everything is OK, you probably will never know it happened. If they believe there is an error, you will receive this letter. You should respond with proof regarding any items you want to claim are justified as fine the way you reported them, or you can just agree to their changes.

- ### REMINDER OF BALANCE DUE
  (FORM CP71A and CP71D)

  This annual notice is provided to you for each tax year that money is still owed. This notice will also inform you of your "Currently Not Collectable" status (CNC).

- ### FINAL NOTICE OF INTENT TO LEVY AND RIGHT TO A HEARING
  (FORM CP90)

  As the notice says, they will levy. The ball is in your court to fix what is wrong—to get into compliance and work out payment arrangements. You have 30 days to appeal the notice of levy. Not any other collection action by the collection division, not the tax in the first place; just the levy.

  You can appeal a lien separately as a lien appeal. You can appeal a collection action with a specific appeal for that. You appeal the tax by an Offer, appeal, or tax court petition. Match your appeals properly.

- ### MATH ERRORS
  (FORM CP101)

  This form consists of math errors they say you made, computational errors, tax deposit errors, no reply to additional information, and so forth. If they are wrong, correct them. If they are right, just ignore the letter.

- ### UNDERPAID TAX
  (FORM CP161)

  This shows the underpaid tax according to the IRS records. Pull your return on assets (ROA) and verify your payments and filing of returns. You will see how the IRS came up with the balance. If you owe it, pay it.

  Use www.eftps.gov if you are set up. Usually, you can call the IRS office listed on the letter to resolve the issue. If you need to do an installment agreement or Offer in Compromise, consult this manual.

- ## PENALTY NOTICE FOR FAILURE TO DEPOSIT
  (FORM CP210 and CP220)

  Check your records against those of the IRS. Check Circular E, and be sure you understand when to make your deposits and how much they should be. You should not rely on IRS notices to tell you how often to deposit.

  You also must use the correct deposit method. Certain large employers must use electronic deposits and not regular bank deposits.

- ## REMINDER OF BALANCE DUE
  (FORM CP501 and CP502)

  These are initial requests before the CP-503 and CP-504 are issued. You are in notice status now. There is likely no collection action yet if this is your only IRS contact. You should consider tackling your IRS debt before they take collection to the next level.

- ## IMPORTANT; IMMEDIATE ACTION REQUIRED
  (CP503)

  If you have received this notice, it means you have ignored the initial tax bill (CP-14), they skipped the CP-501 and CP-502 notices (or you received them prior to this), or your case is back in collections after being declared "Currently Not Collectable" for a while.

  If you owe for more than one tax period, you will receive this notice even if you made arrangements to make installment payments or have been placed in a "hardship" status. It will say on the face of it to ignore it if you have entered into an installment agreement or paid the balance. As long as you have confirmed this, you can ignore the letter.

- ## URGENT WE INTEND TO LEVY ON CERTAIN ASSETS
  (CP504)

  This means you have 30 days before they will actually levy a bank account or wages. If you owe for more than one tax period, you will receive one of these notices for each year.

You may receive this notice even if you have made arrangements to make installment payments or have been placed in a "hardship" status. You may get this notice at any stage of collections. It requires immediate attention. See the chapters on working your case.

- ### REQUEST FOR YOUR TAX RETURN
  (CP515)

  If you have received this notice, it means you have failed to file a tax return, or at least the IRS has not logged in a copy on their computer system. The type of return and tax period will be shown in the upper right corner as well as in the body of the notice.

  File the return as soon as possible; otherwise, your case will be transferred to an audit group, which will prepare the return for you without the deductions you need to lower your liability.

- ### YOUR TAX RETURN IS OVERDUE
  (CP 518)

  Well, now you know. Get it prepared and sent in. If you owe more than you can pay, prepare to deal with the collection division.

- ### INSTALLMENT AGREEMENT PAYMENT NOTICE
  (CP521)

  As long as you are meeting your terms of your payment plan, there is nothing else for you to do. If you've broken your agreement, even if you didn't receive this notice, take the initiative to immediately get back into your agreement.

- ### TWO-YEAR REVIEW FOR MORE FINANCIAL INFORMATION
  (CP522)

  Be careful about responding to this. If your income has gone up, your monthly payments to the IRS will probably go up too. Maybe your living expenses, especially medical, have increased, too.

You want to maximize deductions to offset any increase in income. If you need to lower your monthly payments, argue that, too.

- ### NOTICE OF INTENT TO LEVY
  (CP523)

  Oops, either you defaulted on your agreement or the IRS isn't posting your payments properly. Remember, the IRS must receive payment by the due date of your monthly payments.

  They must also receive payment by the due dates for all taxes you are liable for. Not a day late or a dollar short. In the past, they used to break your agreement and levy your account. Now, they give you about a week to straighten it out. Call and get it fixed.

- ### 30-DAY LETTER TO APPEAL
  (CP525)

  This comes with your audit adjustment letter and gives you 30 days to appeal if you disagree with the adjustments. It's a good idea to prepare this appeal along with your continued arguments and give it to the auditor. This way you protect your rights if you and the auditor disagree about the changes.

- ### NOTICE OF DEFICIENCY
  (CP531)

  This shows how much you owe for each year and how to dispute the adjustments. In many dispute cases, you must pay first and then file a claim for refund. Otherwise you have 90 days to file a tax court petition.

- ### INITIAL CONTACT LETTER ON AN AUDIT
  (CP566)

  Be glad you received it. Many audits take place without taxpayer notification. At least you get a chance upfront to defend your positions. Be sure to prepare properly.

- **WAGE LEVY**
  (Form 668W)

  Fill out the exemption portion so you can get the biggest possible paycheck. This is a very serious collection action. If you want your next full check, you need to take care of delinquent filings and information the IRS needs from you to determine a payback plan right away. Get your information together and "paint a defensible picture" of your financial situation as instructed in this manual.

  File any delinquent returns, and pay any current payments of estimated taxes that are delinquent (or prove that you are not required to make payments by providing your estimated tax calculation).

  Provide this calculation regardless if your payment is less than it normally should be. Then call for an immediate levy release. Give the IRS the name and fax number of the person in your company whose job it is to receive wage levy releases. Your Social Security or retirement can be levied.

- **LEVY**
  (Form 668A)

  Same as above, except this is a one-time bank or financial institution levy. It works on anyone who is holding your money. The funds are on hold for 21 days; then they are sent to the IRS collection person who sent out the levy.

  The back of the levy states that this is a one-time, not continuous, levy. It is only for funds on hand the day it is received.

- **REQUEST FOR CONSIDERATION OF ADDITIONAL FINDINGS**
  (Letter 692)

  This comes with proposed adjustments to your tax return. It gives you courses of action. You can sign it or request an appeal. Be careful; you usually have less than 15 days from your receipt of the letter to take action.

- **FINAL NOTICE OF INTENT TO LEVY**
  (Letter 1058)

  If you received this notice, it means you owe taxes and have ignored Letter 2050. This is one of the most serious collection attempt notices the IRS sends to a taxpayer owing tax.

  It must be responded to or you will lose appeal rights and the IRS will levy anything they can find. As always, prepare a preliminary financial statement so you know where you stand before contacting the IRS.

- **30-DAY LETTER TO PROTEST AN ASSESSMENT ON A 6020B**
  (Letter 1085)

  This is a 30-day letter to protest an IRS tax assessment on a 6020B, which is the IRS code for a payroll report they filled out and filed for you. Don't just accept their figures, even if they are close to the actual amounts.

  Your 941 payroll reports must balance to the 940, the state reports, the W-2s, and so forth. At a minimum, you must see that the total gross wages for the year are the same for each report. Hire a professional to help you if you can't do this on your own.

- **TRUST FUND RECOVERY PENALTY**
  (Letter 1153)

  The remaining FICA and withholding not collected from the business are now being charged to you. Different regions of the country rely on different court rulings to settle some disputes. Basically, you must show that you didn't have authority to direct the company's funds and that you did not have knowledge of the taxes not being paid.

  You should send the RO your appeal along with your proof that you are not liable, just in case they don't agree with you. It shows that you are very serious. Many people will wait on this part until the last minute.

Know that sometimes ROs will chase everyone who has signature authority on the bank account, any stockholder, any signer of a tax form, and any listed officer, and then leave it up to you to defend yourself.

- ### THIRTY DAYS TO PROTEST ON TAX SHELTER
  (Letter 1389)

  This gives you 30 days to protest changes made to your return because of your tax shelter activity. Sign it or appeal it.

- ### WE ARE PROPOSING CHANGES TO YOUR RETURN
  (CP 2000)

  If you received this notice, it means that you have omitted income from your return or that the amount of income or expenses on your return does not match the amount reported to the IRS.

  The following pages will provide an explanation of the changes, followed by a detailed listing of the items that were left off your return or did not match the amounts reported to the IRS. Respond immediately with all the proof you have to sway them to your way of thinking. Do not shortcut your proof.

- ### PLEASE CALL US ABOUT YOUR OVERDUE TAXES OR RETURNS
  (Letter 2050)

  If you received this notice, it means you owe tax and have ignored previous notices CP-504 or CP-523 or you have delinquent tax returns. You may receive this notice even if you have made arrangements to make installment payments or have been placed in a "hardship" status. Do not call. Spend time now preparing the delinquent returns and your financial statements.

- ### PRELIMINARY DETERMINATION LETTER
  (Letter 3016)

  You have 30 days to appeal if they turned down your request for innocent spouse relief. Go back and develop your arguments before calling for a new determination.

If you can't get the reviewer to change to your way of thinking, then file your appeal in a timely manner.

- ## NOTICE OF FEDERAL TAX LIEN FILING AND RIGHT TO A HEARING
  (Letter 3172)

  You now have a real property lien in a particular county only. Just the county listed—not all counties you own property in.

  Some people have sold all their property in other counties and used this money to help them negotiate better payment plans. If the lien will cause a hardship, one acceptable to the IRS, then appeal it.

- ## NOTICE OF LEVY
  (Letter 3174(P)

  This is similar to letter 1058. This form is used when a taxpayer changes address; it requires your immediate attention. You avoid levies by resolving the collection issues or you appeal based on a hardship.

- ## THIRD-PARTY CONTACT
  (Letter 3173)

  This letter advises taxpayers that the IRS may be contacting third parties to ask questions. You can't really do anything about it. Don't worry, though; your personal information will be kept confidential.

- ## NOTICE OF DEFICIENCY
  (Letter 3219)

  This is issued to a taxpayer before an assessment is made and is usually the result of an audit. If you disagree, you need to file a tax court petition within 90 days. You can file an appeal to contest it.

  Don't worry; if you miss the deadline for an appeal, you can usually get Appeals to take the case by filing a tax court petition. Once the IRS legal division accepts your petition, you can call and convince them that this is really a case to be heard by Appeals.

- ## ANNUAL REMINDER NOTICE
  (Letter 3228)

This is a notice of what taxes and years you owe. This is sent yearly as long as there is an unpaid balance.

- ## 30-DAY NOTIFICATION LETTER
  (Letter 3391)

The IRS says you owe for the years stated. This letter describes what the liability is based on. Agree to it or protest. However, if you never filed the return, then file it. Use the numbers that appear in this letter for income and expense, if you feel comfortable with them.

If you just want to accept their information without filing a return, ask for a signature form so you can show you signed the return they prepared. Then file an SFR (substitute for return) using the third-party payer information they have on file.

This includes the W-2s, K-1s, 1099s, etc. filed under your tax ID number. Signing a return and having the IRS enter it in their system will start the statute of limitation on collections.

At times the IRS has collected tax liabilities way beyond ten years because the taxpayer never started the running of the collection statute. The statute starts when the taxpayer files a return that the IRS accepts.

DO YOU WRITE THE IRS?

If you follow this guide, it is unlikely that you will have to write a letter to the IRS unless you are attempting to remove penalties. If you can't get someone at the IRS to take care of your requests by a due date, or if you can't confirm that your request was completed, you may want to send something in writing, certified return receipt, prior to the due date, thereby complying with a statute date that you don't want to expire.

When in doubt, do a mailing to lock in the due date. Never, however, expect it to be read and acted upon in place of your phone calls. Each case will determine the follow-up time for each mailing. Other factors will, too. For example, how much risk are you willing to take that your paycheck or bank account will be levied?

GREAT TAX REDUCTION TECHNIQUE

What if you get a letter from the IRS charging you additional tax based on a math error or a clerical error? How would you like to avoid paying it? Here's how: Communicate back within 60 days and say you request abatement under Section 6213(b)(2). This may get it abated. It's worth a try. Sometimes they reassess it, but they must issue a "notice of deficiency," giving you appeal rights.

Include in the letter a statement that you disagree with the additional tax and the action you want taken, such as "I disagree with the additional tax assessment because I did everything correctly and I want you to remove the taxes." Also state that if they don't remove the taxes, you are requesting that they issue a notice of deficiency so you can file an appeal.

The notice of deficiency will list the changes that they made. (Often you get a correction letter that doesn't spell out why they made the changes in the first place.) Use this approach for letters involving a missing social security number (supply the number and copy of social security card, if you have it, in your letter).

Send your letter to the address they request you respond to. Never be afraid to call or write requesting an explanation of the letter or the adjustments being made.

You may just want to pay the amount charged, or if you are contesting it, you have a better understanding of what you are contesting. If you do call for an explanation, do not give any information as to what you did or why you did anything. They will record it, and it can be used to deny your request for abatement.

PAYMENT PLANS; GETTING ONE THAT WORKS

A CURRENTLY NOT COLLECTABLE (CNC) PAYMENT PLAN

If after you fill out the collection information forms, the IRS can't satisfy the payment of the debt by the end of the statute of limitations on collections, they may put you in a CNC status. This means they have considered any equity in assets as well as your ability to make reasonable monthly payments that will extinguish the debt in a reasonable collection time frame and have concluded that you really don't have the ability to pay.

You should accept this status from them. Make sure it's coded on the system. Then work toward resolving the liability. The liability is still accruing interest and penalties (interest only in a trust fund liability), and you will have to pay it later. Try to set yourself up for an acceptable Offer in Compromise to get rid of the liability. See the chapter on Offers.

STREAMLINED INSTALLMENT AGREEMENT

A Streamlined Installment Agreement does not require the disclosure or verification of financial information. To qualify for a Streamlined Installment Agreement, you must have a tax liability of less than $50,000, and your monthly payments must be made over a period of no more than five years.

This option is much faster than other IRS tax debt resolutions because no IRS managerial approval is required. If you owe more than $50,000, you will have the option of paying a balance below this amount to qualify for a Streamlined Installment Agreement.

INSTALLMENT AGREEMENT REINSTATEMENT FEE

The IRS charges you a fee of $43.00 to reinstate a recently defaulted Installment Agreement. The IRS will usually reinstate delinquent Installment Agreements within three months of the date of the initial request.

APPLICABLE TO ALL INSTALLMENT AGREEMENTS

After obtaining the agreement, don't wait for notices from the IRS to make your payments (a very common mistake). To allow for processing, send the payment in at least 10 days prior to the due date. Immediately after you obtain the agreement, or sooner, in anticipation of the agreement.

Go to www.eftps.com and sign up personally if the agreement is under your social security number. Sign up your business if the liability is under your company's employer identification number. That way you can make sure the payments are processed before the due date.

If you receive subsequent collection notices, they may be for other tax periods. If so, they need to be handled immediately. The agreement can be broken if you owe new taxes, so get this paid off immediately. (Otherwise, you may have to renegotiate your agreement to get it included.)

If the liability existed at the time you made the agreement, it needs to be put into the payment plan. It is essential that all outstanding periods you owe for be put into the agreement when it is negotiated.

If you owe business taxes as well as personal, you may have to get the IRS to do two Installment Agreements. They are often reluctant to do this. An alternative would be to mention how the other account will be handled on the face of the 433D Installment Agreement form.

Occasionally taxpayers have failed to get the IRS to do two agreements and had to liquidate the business to get all the liability under the personal account. Fortunately, the taxpayer saves a lot of money in the process. This is one area in which people often get set up for a fall.

Remember, you must have a plan that corresponds with your current personal and business liabilities as well as any liabilities about to be assessed because of returns not processed yet by the IRS (late or otherwise). This is an area in which we are specialists.

THE WHAT, HOW & WHY OF PENALTIES AND INTEREST

PENALTIES

Removing penalties on your first late personal tax return Form 1040 should be easy. It's pretty much a given. After you pay the liability, you can call and request a penalty removal. Just tell them that you forgot to file on time or that you thought that you had filed. Or you could fill out Form 843 Claim for Refund.

You have to write the form number in and select "Other" on line 3b, though you should still try to prove reasonable cause and not willful negligence.

Use Form 843 for any years of personal returns, or other returns, for which you want to claim penalty abatement.

INTEREST

Interest is charged when there is a balance due. When a tax liability is reduced or abated, the corresponding interest will be too.

When a penalty is abated, the interest on that penalty must be abated too. Interest can be abated if it can be shown that it is attributable in whole or in part to an unreasonable error or delay by an officer or employee of the IRS. You have to prove the following:

1. PROCEDURAL OR MECHANICAL ACT

   The error or delay occurred in connection with "a procedural or mechanical act" or a "managerial act" associated with the case.

2. OCCURRED AFTER CONTACT

   The error or delay occurred after the IRS contacted the taxpayer "in writing" about the case.

3. TAXPAYERS ACTS NOT ATTRIBUTABLE

   No "significant aspect" of the error or delay can be attributed to the taxpayer's actions.

If you want to request relief of interest charged due to an error or delay, do so. It is hard for an honest practitioner to justify charging the fees necessary to defend this, given the odds against it.

Of course, you can try this on your own, but a lot of research will be necessary. You can always appeal a decision against you if the facts are in your favor.

THREE SIMPLE WAYS TO REDUCE YOUR TAX LIABILITY

Pull your Record of Account and make sure the IRS has recorded your payments. Make sure that if they removed any penalties, they took off the related interest. Make sure you file original returns for any years for which they filed a substitute for return (SFR). Make sure you file original reports for any payroll report under code 6020b that the IRS filed.

1. AMEND PRIOR TAX RETURNS

   Any returns that you think are incorrect need to be amended. Submit proof with the return and your copy of the new return and the amended version.

Do not be afraid that this will result in an audit. Submitting your documentation will prove your case, so they will see little opportunity in auditing you.

2. APPLY FOR PENALTY ABATEMENTS

Apply in accordance to the instructions in this book.

PENALTY REMOVAL
MYTHS & REALITIES

REQUESTING RECORDS FROM THE IRS

You can obtain your Record of Account. Currently you can call any number you have for the IRS and have them direct your call accordingly. Another number to use is (859) 669-5498 for transcripts, document 10978, or copies of BMF or IMF accounts; in addition, you can call (866) 860-4259 if you prefer calling toll free. Numbers change, however.

With a signed Power of Attorney, anyone authorized on your power of attorney can pull your transcripts in three days.

Should you pull your Individual Master File (IMF) or Business Master File (BMF)?

Unless you are going to court to prove certain documentation (which is not recommended), it is best that you not pull any of these. If you need such documentation to look something up, your RO will generally be happy to fax you his or her copy.

What you should pull is the "Record of Account" transcripts. These provide information regarding when certain transactions took place, including the date a return was received from the taxpayer or made up by the IRS.

The Record of Account also records dates of payments, credits, interest charges, penalty charges, statute write offs, Offer in Compromise filings, bankruptcy filings, and so on. These records are usually comprehensive enough to solve your IRS problems. Pull them whenever you are resolving what you owe for any year.

Many people use the IRS letters as a reference for what they owe. The problem with doing this is that the information in the letters is often incomplete and out of date. Your "Record of Account" should contain the complete story of your tax situation.

Make sure the Record of Account reflects what actually exists; otherwise, you will overpay, or you will mistakenly think that you don't owe, do nothing about it, and then wind up with a wage levy.

Make it your responsibility to see that the Record of Account is correct. Look up any codes you don't understand on the IRS web site. You can always call IRS Automated Collections System general numbers at 1-800-829-7650 or 1-800-829-1040 to request documents.

PENALTY REMOVAL

If you don't want to pay the penalties pertaining to a particular year or period, you can file an 843 claim for refund, if applicable (read the instructions). Usually you can get the penalties off for the first period involved, after paying it in full, just by asking. Show that it was due to reasonable cause and not willful negligence.

The IRS looks for specific wording. Consult the IRS penalty handbook for further information.

HOW TO FILL OUT FORM 843

1. Fill out name and address and so on. List the start and end of each period. Example, 1/1/05–12/31/05 for 2005 1040. Use a separate form for each period.

2. Copy the amount from the notice.

3. Type of tax or penalty and the form number. For the form 1040, select "other" and write it in.

4. If not just interest and penalty from IRS error (not in this case) just leave blank.

5. Put "see attached" and attach your letter. Fill out the signature and date portion. Make a copy. Mail it certified return receipt. Mark your calendar to follow up about six weeks to see if it has been processed. As with all correspondence to the IRS, take responsibility to work it through the system.

If you can't agree with Automated Collections System, you should request that the case be sent to an RO. You can tell them that you want to deal with someone face to face, someone local who knows what the local living expenses are.

ROs are better able to make decisions concerning your 433A and 433B and the monthly payments you are to make to pay off your debt. You may have to call back a few times to get this.

Each time you call back, keep trying to get the payment amount you want. Remember to argue within the guidelines given to you. Do not argue for favors because of your hardship situation. Keep supporting your reasons for them to accept your income and expense items so that you will pay the monthly amount that you figured you should pay.

If they still don't agree, request that the case go out to a local RO. Tell them that you will make the monthly payment that you are trying to get (the first one now if necessary), demonstrating that you are not asking that it go to a RO as a stalling tactic.

If you get a lot of resistance, rethink your strategy. You may be holding out for an expense deduction that won't stop you from meeting the monthly payment amount anyway.

MORE PENALTY REMOVAL

Failure to File Penalty Code 6651. Check the penalty handbook for the reasons to address removal of this penalty. Some of the most common ones are the following:

You mailed returns and payments in a timely manner, used the wrong address, relied on information from the IRS, had an illness or death in the family, were a victim of a fire or flood, couldn't get the information to file on time, were given wrong advice by an attorney, and so on. Prepare as you would a regular affidavit.

This is a big penalty (5% per month) of the tax liability for up to five months from the date the return was due. So let's say you owe $1,500,000 as of the due date. Then two months later you pay the whole thing but do not file the return until eight months later.

You may think that the penalty is only for two months because the liability was paid off. How can they charge a penalty based on a liability that doesn't exist anymore? Well the IRS says they can.

NEGLIGENCE AND SUBSTANTIAL UNDERSTATEMENT PENALTIES

IRS Code 6662 and Code 6664. The IRS will charge this penalty in addition to late filing and late paying penalties. They charge it for negligence or intentional disregard of the rules or regulations and for substantially understating the tax liability.

You can't be reckless when preparing your return. This is why you should choose your tax preparer wisely. You could pay penalties that amount to far more than any savings in preparation fees. These are easier to beat than the other penalties.

1. Consult the IRS penalty handbook.
2. Demonstrate in affidavit form that the above situation does not exist.

AUDIT APPEALS

Try to work with your auditor and his or her manager. The purpose of audit appeals is usually to bail out people who missed audit appointments or who were uncooperative during the audit.

Most auditors (unlike the collection division) tend to be very logical and understanding about your situation. Audit appeals are a little looser than the appeal mentioned below for trust fund.

These auditors understand that not everyone has an adequate chance to provide the necessary documents to avoid adjustments against them. Do the following:

1. File a timely appeal. Read the instructions carefully. You have 90 days if issued a notice of deficiency; otherwise, you have 30 days.

2. Look up the tax law involving the items disallowed or added to the return. Become familiar with the reasons an item may not be accepted, and prepare to defend it.

3. As with all appeals, look up cases that support any items you think may be a problem, and obtain notarized statements from anyone who can support your claims.

APPEAL OF THE TRUST FUND OR CIVIL PENALTY

If you can't convince the RO that you are not liable, you must file an appeal before the 30 days are up. An appeal should cite the court cases and other documentation that went into your research, but if time is running out, you can file a short summary version with a request that a more detailed version be permitted to follow later.

This is an area that relies heavily on court decisions in your region of the country. Find out what federal circuit court your state is in, and pay attention to decisions in your favor from that circuit.

You will have to do the following to win. (Remember that if the RO and manager didn't agree with you, they feel that they have a case.)

1. Become familiar with exactly what constitutes liability for the trust fund.

2. Find out how the courts in your circuit tend to distinguish items that make someone liable.

3. File your appeal, even the short version, on time and with as much detail as you can so it isn't turned down.

4. When the Appeals conference is scheduled, call up and request to look at the files they have. This is your right, and they don't mind, so be sure to do it whenever you file an Appeal.

5. Make sure you do a lot of case research. Appeals are looking for you to prove that if they error, you will win in court. That is their main objective, so you may as well know it now. This is not an appeal for sympathy based on hardship. This is a question of you being able to prove to them that if they still want to make you liable, it will be a waste of the IRS's time and money to take you to court because you will win.

6. Don't forget witnesses. Get signed, notarized statements from people who worked with you and have firsthand knowledge of anything that helps prove your case.

IT IS HIGHLY RECOMMENDED THAT YOU HIRE A PROFESSIONAL REPRESENTATIVE WHEN APPEALING WITH THE TRUST FUND.

INDEPENDENT CONTRACTOR DISPUTES

If the IRS is trying to say you paid someone contract labor (no withholding tax taken out) instead of on a salary (withholding tax taken out) and you feel that you are in the right, you should fight it.

Proof can be found by using your local state's unemployment or workforce office's rules for determining whether or not someone should/could be paid contract labor. Document in detail how you meet the tests just as you normally would when preparing an affidavit. Get signed affidavits from as many witnesses as you can who will say that they witnessed your actions as a contract labor person, not an employee, according to the rules. Do this within the 30-day time period.

Look up the current safe harbor rules to avoid the IRS charging you for several years if you had a reasonable basis for treating them as contract and filed all the applicable 1099s on time.

Remember: Even if you lose and are charged the self-employment tax, interest, and penalties, none of it is trust fund (because you never took it out of the paycheck in the first place). Therefore, if you have a corporation or LLC, you will have time to set yourself up to liquidate the company if the taxes are too much for you to handle.

A corporate liquidation will get you out of all of these. You can call or email us to see if you qualify. If you don't qualify, we can look at ways you can qualify in the near future.

WAGE LEVIES - BANK LEVIES

Reasons the IRS may remove levies are the following:

1. Statute of limitations on collections has expired

2. Releasing the levy makes their collection easier

3. The IRS is convinced that the levy creates a severe economic hardship for you

However, the best thing to do is accelerate the collection process. Money can go toward the first payment that you negotiate 45 days from now, so the next payment isn't due for two and a half months! The IRS will give back money from a bank levy, allowing the bank to cash certain checks written to employees who are not part of your immediate family.

You should also argue that the money frozen in the bank was your federal tax deposit money, so it should be coded to that before the payment of any back taxes.

If you can negotiate the removal of these levies with the agreement that the money go toward the first installment payment 45 days from now, this will give you two and a half months before you have to write a check toward the back taxes. See Chapter 8 for advice on payment plans.

AFFIDAVITS

Signed affidavits switch the burden of proof back to the IRS. Sometimes that doesn't matter, but many times it does. Here is a general outline:

Affidavits need to be exact as to facts and conclusions, so make sure you include the following:

1. Reference the letter from the IRS that you received, with the title and name of the letter. Include the date that appears on the top of the letter.

2. State specifically what aspect of the letter you take objection to. Then state your objection. For example, if the letter imposes a tax, don't state the reasons you can't pay the tax.

   State the reasons you object to the tax being applied to you. For example, you filed your return. You already paid the tax. The code doesn't allow the penalty to be applied because of a certain reason, and so on. Keep it short, sweet, and to the point.

3. State all facts and leave out emotions. Include the events that led up to the actions you took. State why you took them and how your actions were the only prudent choice.

   Show that this was an issue of reasonable cause, not willful neglect. Show that your actions were in good faith; any failure to pay was a result of prudence when providing for payment and that you still were unable to pay without suffering a hardship.

4. In many cases, there is a set of reasons you have to prove in order to use an affidavit. Google "IRS penalty handbook" and look up "relief from penalties." You will find the definitions needed to get out of penalties.

5. When asking that penalties be removed, make sure that you ask separately for any interest to be removed. Sometimes the IRS removes penalties and forgets to remove the interest that has accrued on those penalties.

6. Put your declaration at the bottom of the letter. Use words such as "I swear under penalties of perjury that to the best of my knowledge, the above facts contained in this letter are true and complete." Sign and date the letter.

THE IRS IS MISSING A RETURN YOU FILED

Sometimes the IRS is missing a return you are certain you filed. If you want credit for filing it on the date you did so, prepare a letter (affidavit), stating the exact situation. For example, "*On March 4, 2001, I personally went to the mailbox at the post office at 2348 Main St., Buffalo, New York, and dropped in an envelope containing my 2006 Form 1040 personal income tax return, sealed and addressed to the IRS at 1200 Government Plaza, Albany, New York.*"

Include any proof of mailing that you may have. Have your letter notarized, and give it or mail it to the collection officer. If no one is assigned your case, mail it directly to the IRS address designated in the letter you received informing you of the missing return.

If you found out by pulling your own Record of Account, then call Automated Collections System to find out the status of your case and who to mail it to.

By now you should know to Google "IRS Automated Collections System PHONE NUMBER," or something like that. The numbers they give are (800) 829-1040 and (800) 829-4933. You can always call phone numbers on other IRS letters you have, and they can direct you as well. Always send any mailing to the IRS certified, return receipt.

To make sure you win when it comes up in the future, send all correspondence to the IRS certified, return receipt, after making a copy for yourself of every document you send. Staple it all together so you have an exact duplicate of the order of each paper sent.

Mail each tax return copy. You keep the originals, including signature pages, in a separate envelope. A photocopy of a signature is as good as an original in most cases.

If sending in 1040s for more than three years, mail each one three days apart. That should keep it from going to the fraud division to determine whether they should question why so many returns are delinquent.

IRS LETTER CHARGING UNREPORTED INCOME

Just get a copy of the third-party payer information. Call the IRS to obtain a transcript. Very often the notice will list the income sources and amounts, so you may be able to verify it right away. This is a correction notice, so this is good news, and you can contest it.

You can state that each source individually are not your income (or only part of it), and swear that you didn't omit income on your return. Then request that under code section 6213(b), they must abate the liability, or in the case where they elect not to abate it, they must send you a notice of deficiency so that you can file an appeal.

Then state under penalties of perjury that you declare that the facts stated in this letter are true, correct, and complete. Of course, it is not advised that you do this if the facts are not true.

Follow the procedures outlined above for preparing an affidavit. You should also include Form 843 Claim for Refund and Request for Abatement. This will formalize your abatement request. You have to change the form a bit. Above the words "Claim for Refund," put "Abatement request under code section 6213(b)."

At worst, if they don't accept this and issue the 90-day notice of deficiency, you can continue to make sure they add only the correct amount to your liability. Try to get the IRS to remove any negligence or substantial understatement penalties.

After you pay it off, you can file a claim for refund of taxes paid (same form). Explain that you didn't realize you had this income in the first place and that you will endeavor to keep better records in the future.

Do not "MESS" with your money and your future by representing yourself before the IRS. Get professional help by calling (800) 838-6665 or email info@tax-help.com

CRITICAL FORMS; HOW AND WHEN TO FILL THEM OUT

FORM 433A

Things to remember:

1. Each numbered section must have a response. If the answer is zero, put zero. If the question is not applicable to your situation, then put N/A for "not applicable." Just make sure all items are answered. If you don't know the answer, then find it! If you can't find it, then estimate the answer to the best of your ability.

    Do not round off all your answers. The IRS will not guess or even estimate your income and expenses. They expect you to gather source documents to arrive at the numbers you use. You can use this to your advantage, putting together a group of months that support the lowest monthly payment you want to make.

2. You must try to get a monthly payment low enough that you can pay it on time each month. You always have the option of paying more money so the balance can be paid off sooner (saving interest and penalties). However, be aware that no matter how much you prepay the liability, you absolutely must pay the total amount of your monthly payment on time or you will default the Installment Agreement.

    Under recent rules, the IRS will give you a short time (perhaps a week) to pay and "catch up" the agreement. But don't rely on it. Even though administratively they are not taking action, technically if you file or pay late (details under another section), you broke the agreement.

Once that happens, they can take collection action whenever they want to do so. We have never seen or heard of the IRS taking collection action (levying or seizing) when all five parts of an agreement are still in force. They are as follows:

- An IRS manager must approve an agreement.

- The agreement is given a status code, such as the number 60 or 63.

- The taxpayer files all business and personal returns on time, including any valid extensions.

- All taxes the taxpayer is involved with are paid on time. The payments must be coded in the IRS's computer by the correct due dates. It does not matter whether an exemption to the penalties is met. Payments must meet the quarterly estimate rules if there is not enough withholding from paychecks.

- Monthly installment payments must be coded in the IRS's computer by the due date, and for the full amount.

3. Propose of this form. The IRS uses Form 433A to see what income is available to make monthly payments. They also use it to see what assets you have and how they can access your assets if they need/want to levy or seize them.

You will use this form to show the IRS that you don't have much to give them and why they should accept a low dollar payment plan or Offer in Compromise.

INSTRUCTIONS

Each item is numbered from 1 to 45. Each numbered item must have a response. Use N/A (for not applicable), zero, or none as appropriate.

Read each numbered item carefully. You will be painting a picture of your ability to pay your tax liability.

1. Put in your name and other required information. Try not to use a P.O. Box unless that address conforms with the IRS's records, such as the Record of Account.

2. Marital status. Use married and separated if separated (living in different households) but still married.

3. Social security number. Use the one the IRS has and your date of birth.

4. Same for spouse.

5. Own home, rent, and so on. Remember to always think of your purpose when answering questions. Paint a picture that supports your purpose, and be sure it makes sense. If living together, the IRS will consider both incomes and apply the joint living expenses to arrive at a monthly payment.

   If living apart and not sharing income and expenses, they may only allow the expenses for one person. If living apart and still sharing income and expenses, you will have to argue the additional living expenses created by the two households.

6. Dependents are people you are obligated to support. Use the income tax guide definitions for blood relatives. If they are not living with you, they won't be allowed under table allowances except for legally obligated additional expenses you incur.

   The most common situation of a dependent not living with you would be your minor child living with your ex-spouse (for whom you meet the dependency test). No problem—your child support and other court-ordered payments will be deductible.

   Your goodwill for paying child support outside of a court order hurts you when dealing with the collection division. You could go back to court and raise your court-ordered payments. This is a good idea. As long as it's a court order for child support and related child welfare, and you can prove that you are making the payments, the IRS does not generally deny the expense when doing a payment plan or Offer.

7. If you operate a business, put the information here. Then fill out Form 433B so you can deduct your related expenses against the income.

8. If you or your spouse receives 1099s (for contract income, not interest and/ or dividends), put it on a 433B. If you don't claim any expenses against the income, then you can leave it here.

   Income from W2-s goes here. Remember to include the requested attachments unless you elect to show proof in a different way, such as over more months then the three requested.

9. See above ^

10. List the other sources of income. If any income is temporary (a few months or so), be sure to include it on page 6 with an explanation that you won't have that income available to you anymore.

11. List your checking account and balance. If the balance is high because of outstanding checks, then put a lower amount down. Submit bank reconciliations to the IRS showing that the balance is always lower after the checks are cashed. You can argue and win the lower amount.

12. List your other accounts. Same rules as #11 apply.

13. List your investments. If they are tied up as collateral, the IRS can't expect you to cash them in and pay them.

14. Cash on hand. Hopefully you don't have much. Notice the shaded totals for section 5. They will be added up later as available assets for the IRS. The internal revenue manual, in the collections section, tells the revenue officer to clean out all available assets before considering an installment agreement. All of your assets, cash or otherwise, get added together and increase the amount you have to pay in Offer.

15. Available credit. Don't worry; it's credit, not your money. The IRS will look for untapped sources for you to use and pay them faster.

16. If you have a cash value in your life insurance policy, they will likely ask you to withdraw it.

17. Other information. This helps the IRS know about the availability of assets for their taking and other things that will/may affect your ability to pay the liability and make timely payments.

18. List all the vehicles titled in your spouse's and your names. Guess at any balances that you can't supply in a timely manner. Remember, if you are really pressed for time, it's better to leave out some information than to fight with an IRS employee to get more time.

19. You may want to save that first extension of time request for when you really can't meet a deadline. Getting more than one extension of time is an art for experienced representatives and taxpayers with a good gift for eliciting empathy.

20. If you lease (or lease to own), put the vehicles here.

21. List real estate in your name. Fill in all items and attach an explanation for any fractional or joint ownership. If real estate is not in your name, don't list it. But remember, if you have an equity interest in a corporation, partnership, family trust, and so on, you must list it on this form.

    You will be signing the bottom of the last page "under penalties of perjury" so on the day you sign it, the information must be true, correct, and complete to the best of your knowledge.

    If you have a greater than 50% ownership interest in an asset or business, put it on 433A or 433B as appropriate, with a value for your interest. Be prepared to defend it. Some people with small value assets or small value interests leave it off altogether. If the value is minimal, you don't have to worry about fraud, but recording it allows you to avoid the argument concerning valuation.

    Be careful about interests that are traceable, such as information on a K-1 from Form 1065 or 1120S that the IRS has access to. Be extra careful in an Offer. If the Offer division feels that you are hiding assets, they can turn down your Offer based on that. In fact they can and do find excuses quite readily for turning down offers.

22. Use quick sale value for current value.

23. This should be on 433B. If you are paid on a 1099 with no deductions for related expenses (it's rare not to have expenses) and decided not to use form 433B, but actually have some business assets, list them here. Does it matter where you list it? In general, no. However, in an offer situation, you are allowed to deduct an amount as little as $3,000 from your business assets.

24. A/R-I always leave blank. You could put down people who owe you money personally if you want the IRS to attempt to collect it. Business A/R goes on the 433B.

25. Wages are from W-2s only.

26. See above ^

27. Interest and dividends (from your cash accounts). Of course if you liquidated them, or will do shortly, the interest and dividends won't exist anymore, so leave it blank.

28. Carryover from 433B (or 1099 total if 433B is not used).

29. If you actually happened to get income from a rental, (pull out depreciation; it's not a cash outlay), put it here or explain why you won't have any income anymore so they can't add it to your other income.

30. Pensions and Social Security go here.

31. See above ^

32. Child support you receive. Yes it's income—for collection purposes anyway. Don't worry; you will get deductions to offset this.

33. Alimony goes here.

34. List other income. (So now, don't you feel rich after adding up your many sources of income?)

35. See above previous question.

And now, for your best creative effort to offset that large amount of income, show the IRS that most of your income is absolutely necessary for your living expenses.

The first three have table amounts. It's almost impossible to get the IRS to go beyond these amounts. Download the tables from the IRS website.

36. Food. They will accept at least the table amount, even if you spend less. If you have a physician's letter requiring you to eat certain foods that increase your food bill, you can add that to your health expense.

37. Make sure you include the letter with your receipts. Read the items in the center of the page that explains what to include on the lines that have the postscripts numbered 1-7.1-3 pertaining to income and 4-7 pertaining to expenses.

38. Housing and utilities. Table amount again, but they have a one-year rule, so if your amount is greater than the table amount, you can use your amount for the first year, and then their smaller table amount after that. They claim it's not automatically given at your request, but they will let you have what you can prove is needed.

39. Use the table for each vehicle. There are two parts: one for payment and one for the operating expenses. These amounts are capped, so read the instructions carefully.

40. Medical expenses from your paycheck, separate payments, and any other methods you actually paid for physicians, dentists, insurance, travel to physicians, prescriptions, and all medical-related expenses. Be prepared with receipts and an explanation of why the past expenses represent the future!

41. This is your income, FICA, and Medicare from your paychecks and estimated payments. Many people, including the IRS, just take this from the last filed income tax return, and divide by twelve to get the monthly amount.

    If that gives you a larger deduction, don't argue with them. If not, then do an estimated tax calculation based on the year-to-date income and expenses. You may need your accountant to help you.

42. Child support and other court-ordered payments go here and are readily accepted by the IRS.

43. Childcare is allowed only if both spouses work. Special needs dependent care and expenses tend to be OK even if one spouse doesn't have income.

44. Life insurance. You might have a hard time getting the IRS to accept this.

45. Other secured debt, yes, under acceptable circumstances.

46. Other expenses. If you have certain expenses that are necessary for living and are not part of any item above, then list them here and be prepared to argue aggressively.

Now, #34 less #35 shows how much you can pay each month toward your liability. Let's look at this from another perspective. Let's say you have a liability of approximately $50,000 under your social security number for personal and/or trust fund taxes. Consider the following cases:

1. You hardly have any assets (maybe $5,000 worth), and your 433A shows that you can't make monthly payments. You are probably an Offer in Compromise candidate. If you fill out the offer form prior to the deadline given to you by the IRS collection person and meet the other requirements, then submit the Offer to the IRS in place of doing a payment plan.

   If you can't submit it by the deadline, give them the 433A and/or 433B information with backup, and request time to do an Offer. You should be able to get it.

2. You hardly have any assets (maybe $5,000 worth), and you can pay $300–$400 per month. Given that the $50,000 is accruing interest and penalties, you will not be able to pay this off in 10 years.

   Ten years is the (statute of collections) time that the IRS has to collect the money starting from the date it is assessed, not that they will give you that amount of time anyway.

   They want the liability paid off as soon as the financial statements allow. (In the alternative, at least three to five years.) You are probably an Offer candidate.

   Fill out the Offer form prior to the deadline given to you by the IRS collection person and be sure you meet the other requirements; then submit the offer to the IRS in place of doing a payments plan. If you can't submit it by the deadline, give them the 433A and/or 433B information with backup and request time to do an Offer. You should be able to get it.

3. You hardly have any assets (maybe $5,000 worth), and you can pay $1,000 per month. This is close. You're probably not an Offer candidate, but you will have to argue a longer payout, probably by signing a 2751 extension, giving them additional time, past the statute of limitations on collections, to collect the money. You should agree to this so you can get your payment plan or offer.

4. You hardly have any assets (maybe $5,000 worth), and you can pay $1,000–$2,000 per month; move forward with the agreement or Offer. But wait, even though the financial statements say so, you really can't afford $1,000 per month.

   Well, too bad, says the IRS. You do not have a choice. If you don't agree, they will take levy and seizure action till the debt is paid! This is why you always seek to have a binding Agreement or an accepted Offer.

It is your job, before you turn in the 433A and 433B, to show or "paint the picture" of the lowest monthly payment amount and least asset liquidation that you can afford. It is okay to liquidate more assets, such as your home as well. It will lower all the interest and penalties that are accruing. If you want to pay a larger monthly payment, then do so at your option. You don't want to be obligated to pay more than the minimum you can afford.

FORM 433B

1. Each numbered section must have a response. If the answer is zero, put zero. If the question is not applicable to your situation, then put N/A for not applicable. Just make sure all items are answered. If you don't know the answer, then find it! If you can't find it, then estimate it to the best of your ability.

2. Do not round off all your answers. The IRS doesn't want you to guess or even estimate your income and expenses. They expect you to gather source documents to arrive at the numbers you use. You can use this to your advantage, putting together a group of months that support the lowest monthly payment you want to make.

3. Purpose of this form—the IRS uses it to see what income is available to make monthly payments for a business agreement or to be added to the form 433A to increase income. They also use it to see what assets you have and how they can get to it if they need/want to seize it! You will use this form to show them that you don't have much to give them and why they should accept a low dollar payment plan or an Offer in Compromise.

Use this form to show income from a business that is not on a W-2, such as income shown on a 1099. If your income is on a K-1 and you have expenses against that income (not already included on the K-1), then use this form to deduct those expenses. Always check back to your 1040 income tax return.

Sometimes you have business expenses included on a schedule C, Form 2106, office in home, and so on that you want to include on the 433B. If the form doesn't show where to include the expense, just attach a separate sheet of paper.

INSTRUCTIONS

Each item is numbered; the numbers are 1–39. Each numbered item must have a response. Use N/A, zero, or none, as appropriate.

Read each numbered item carefully. You will be painting a picture of your ability to pay your tax liability.

1. Name, address, etc. If same as residence, put that address.

2. Employer identification number, if you have one, even if you don't currently have employees. Otherwise put N/A on line 2a. Line 2b is for the type of entity. This can be a sole proprietor, incorrectly referred to as a DBA (Doing Business As). Corporations have DBAs too! If you just get paid on a 1099 and don't really operate a separate business, check "Other" and write "none."

   Don't worry if you are paid on a 1099, or even if you don't file a 1099 for your income, when it should be correctly reported on a W-2. They need to have the correct picture of your income reporting.

Let the collection person tell you how it should be filed. They actually enjoy helping people get into compliance with the correct report filing. It is rare that they report it to the audit division, especially if you start correcting the reporting and tax-paying error immediately.

3. Put your name as the contact name—or the name of your spouse or child. Use whoever will be speaking to the IRS for you. Don't put the name of your power of attorney, if you assigned one on form 2848 (not 4828), if they are not actively representing you. If you do, the IRS will call that person. They ask for an email even though no IRS collection employees contact taxpayers or representatives by email.

4. Always indicate the owner or majority shareholder, even if the actual banking functions are delegated to another employee. Until you've resolved who is liable for the trust fund, it's best not to mention other employees.

5. Same principle as #4. Limit this to owners and someone with signature authority on the bank account. You can resolve missing information later.

6. Be careful here. If you are in a "hostile" situation and feel they will immediately go after your accounts receivable, you can leave some out or indicate that you need more time to complete the form. Don't sign the 433B. If you do, put a comment near your signature that the form is not complete. (Incidentally, people are not generally charged with breaking the law for leaving out their A/R and signing the form.)

As to contracts awarded but not stated, an A/R or notes receivable is money actually owed to you on the day that the 433B is signed and dated. This is one sensitive area in which people representing themselves might need to hire a professional.

An experienced professional can keep the IRS at bay while simultaneously keeping you and the representative out of trouble. There's an art to striking a good balance between collecting A/R and stopping IRS collection action. Use page 6 if needed, or attach a separate schedule.

Many ROs get mad if you leave out the A/R, so expect them to accuse you of hiding them. Of course that is what you are doing when you leave it out (some people just forget or are sloppy preparers of forms), so don't leave it out unless you are very scared and think that you can collect it within a few weeks. In most cases, if you cooperate with the IRS, it is unlikely that they will levy your A/R.

Levies come when you miss a deadline the collection person gives you or if you continue to file late returns and make late payments. It is rare for an IRS collection employee to give you a deadline and then issue a levy before the deadline. However, a levy may have been issued prior to your conversation in which you were given a deadline; always ask, "Are there any levies pending now?" Tell them you want to make sure nothing happens before the deadline.

7. Just answers based on what you know, and guess on the amount you don't know and can't look up. If you are filing an Offer in Compromise, or even a payment plan, the bankruptcy question is very important. They must make sure the bankruptcy was dismissed (turned down) or discharged (the plan was accepted and completed), before the IRS can continue your collection case.

8. List your vehicles titled in the company name. Those titled in your personal name get listed on the 433A. If you are a sole proprietor and have vehicles used for business purposes more than 50% of the time, list them here. Some IRS collection employees may want them listed here even for less than 50% use. Don't sweat this; it's not that important.

9. Same as #8 for leased vehicles.

10. List real estate titled in the company name. Real estate titled in your individual name is put on 433A. It doesn't matter if it is used solely in your business. A word of caution here. Let's say that you have a corporation or LLC and have a vehicle or real estate used 100% for business but titled in the personal name. It is not a business-owned asset! Even though you put it on the corporate return and depreciate it, it is still a personal asset for IRS collection purposes.

Do not be intimidated. This comes into play mainly if you are liquidating your corporation. Personal assets can be seized only to offset personal liabilities—IRS liabilities on your IMF account under your social security number, mostly made up of Form 1040 personal income tax and trust fund tax.

11. Same as #8. Be careful to list your payment and final dates throughout this form.

12. Does the company have investments? Personal investments go on the 433A.

13. List the company's separate accounts, showing the balance after all outstanding checks are cleared. Otherwise the IRS will want this money. It will also increase the offer amount if you are doing an offer. This is another area often argued by a representative.

    If you want the IRS to use a lower amount, you will need to show that you have clients who don't cash their checks right away. You then show that the balance is always lower after they have cashed their checks.

14. List other accounts you have. Remember that you will be asked to give this money to the IRS before they even consider the monthly payment plan. So if you want to keep the interest and penalties down, liquidate your accounts and pay them off.

    On the other hand, if you feel that you won't be able to pay the monthly amount they will request, cash in some of your accounts and don't list them. If they ask about it, you can say (if you actually did) that it went toward your basic living expenses. Again, this is a big negotiation area. Don't get greedy here. Obviously an account that has a lot more money than what could pay your living expenses should be used partially for that, and the rest to pay toward your tax liability.

    Don't try to hide things from the IRS. Once you agree that you owe the money (with any pending adjustments that will be made later), it's best to pay them off as soon as possible.

    Make sure your Record of Account for each liability period is cleared, and be done with the collection division of the IRS. The only reason to try to "hold back" is to use money to pay the monthly amount that the IRS wants you to pay. This is just in case you are short each month.

    For example, suppose you feel that the most you can pay is $700 per month. The IRS says you should pay $1,000. This is an extra $300 per month, or $3,600 per year. Instead of fighting, going to the manager, filing an appeal, contacting the Taxpayer Advocate, etc., it's a lot easier to have backup money to use to make up the monthly difference.

You can always turn down the overtime work and extra clients till after the payment plan is approved.

15. If you have available credit, the IRS may expect you to tap this source. Not a bad idea. The interest rates will usually be less than the IRS's interest plus penalty rates.

16. Fill in the period you are using. If showing one month of income and expenses below, put the monthly period here. If you are using more than one month, cross out the words "gross monthly" and "actual monthly" below, and then write in the period (e.g., three months or one year).

    When you finish line 39, you will subtract line 39 from line 26 and divide it by the number of months in the period you are using. Then carry that amount to form 433A if you are submitting that. This difference should be the income minus expenses you have available each month.

17. (Items 18 to 39) Instead of trying to fit your whole income statement here, you can just write, "see attached." Remember to make sure your bank statements and receipts reflect this, or you will have a lot of explaining to do later. Better to explain now and steer the IRS to your way of thinking.

IRS TRAP

Making additional payments or increasing your monthly payment voluntarily doesn't result in a reduction in your next monthly payment. For example, suppose you are required to pay $500 per month. One month you get "extra money" and pay an extra $10,000. The next month, you can only pay $450 (not the whole $500).

Paying only $450 breaks your agreement. If this ever happens, or if you are short on a payment, call the IRS and tell them that you will be short; they will give you permission to pay later. You still technically broke your agreement, and the IRS can take collection action anytime they want; however, it is rare for them to do so.

FORM 433F

Most IRS collection personnel want you to fill out the 433A to present your personal income and expenses, and a 433B to present your (non-salaried or non-W-2) income and related expenses, assets, and liabilities. Sometimes Automated Collections System will demand that you fill out and send in the 433F form.

Map everything out on the 433A (and if needed, on the 433B), figure out your table allowances, and get an idea of what your monthly payment should be. Then transfer that information to the 433F. Put anything that doesn't fit on a separate attached sheet. You are entitled to all IRS allowable expenses regardless of whether you can fit them on the forms! Then do your formal request for an Installment Agreement in a separate letter and include it with Form 433F and the required backup.

Remember, even if they ask for three months of receipts, ask yourself whether three months gives an accurate description of what you can pay each month. If you extend the receipts to four months, five or six will that give you less income or more expenses because of additional recurring medical bills paid?

Also, document your expenses with the most extensive amount of backup receipts, cancelled checks, doctors' letters, and so on. And then ask yourself—if you gave it to the high school kid next door, would she understand what you are trying to say? Will she think your support proves you actually paid what you are saying you did?

This form is very similar to the 433A; please refer the previous explanations for instructions on filling it out.

JOINT TAX RETURNS AND YOUR INNOCENT SPOUSE

There are now many court decisions under the applicable code section 6015. Look up cases to support your request when filing and be sure to check any updates to the code.

If this gets really difficult to handle and you can't afford to hire a good representative, try to convince the Taxpayer Advocate's office to help you (scream hardship) or your current RO. Some ROs are really very nice and may help you. Just don't dump it on their lap. Put together what you can, and ask them to review it. Write down specific questions for them to answer so that you can complete it.

Of course, if you didn't sign the return, then you are not liable. If you had income, then you always had the choice to file under the filing status of "married filing separate." Separate returns means you pay your share and he pays his. Community property states split income, so that may cause a problem for the lower-income spouse.

THREE SOURCES OF RELIEF IF YOU SIGNED A JOINT RETURN:

1. Code 6015(b) is a general relief rule (IRS must prove) for joint filers, even if the filers are still married (if still married, it's even harder to win your claim).

   Under 6015(b)(1), you must prove that all five conditions are met. List them one by one and explain how they are met. It is essential that you try to show evidence rather than simply making statements.

   • You filed a joint return. (A copy of the return is good.)

- There is an understatement of tax on a joint return attributable to errors of the other spouse. A copy of the return showing a liability would qualify, or you can show that the liability was the result of an audit. Then show that it was from his income and deductions and not from yours.

- Show that when you signed the return, you did not know or have reason to know of the understatement of the tax. Here is where they get you. If there was a refund or a small liability on the bottom line, or the taxes were a result of an audit, this is less difficult to prove. But if the big liability you are trying to get out of is staring at you on the bottom of the second page of Form 1040, not far from where you put your signature, you will have a big fight from the IRS if you try to prove you didn't know that the taxes were owed.

  Different parts of the country have different interpretations of this. It is important to do your case research. The knowledge part should be satisfied if you did not know or have reason to know at the time the return was signed that the taxes would not be paid. You must establish that it was reasonable to believe he would pay the liability.

- It is inequitable to hold you liable for the joint tax. (Here you show not only that it is his but also that you never benefited from the money. If he bought you fancy clothes, a new car, a house, and so forth with the money, then the IRS will want you to pay the tax on it.)

- You must show that you are making this claim within two years after the IRS first began collection activities. (Call Automated Collections System or your RO right away to have them look up this date for you. Then you will know when the two years are up.)

2. Code 6015(c) provides additional relief for joint filers who at the time of the election (now, while you are filing for innocent spouse):

   - Are divorced or legally separated from the other tax return signing party.

   - Have lived apart from the other party for the preceding twelve months.

Under 6015(c), to deny the claim, the IRS must prove that you had actual knowledge of the terms that gave rise to the deficiency at the time you signed the return. If you knew of some of the deductions, then that part will be denied but not the rest.

3. If code 6015(b) or (c) doesn't apply, you still can obtain relief under code 6015(f).

Here you show that even if you don't qualify under the above codes, it would be inequitable to hold you liable. You should get signed, notarized statements from unrelated parties. You must satisfy all of the following conditions:

1. You filed a joint return for the year in question.

2. You don't qualify under 6020(b) or 6020(c).

3. You must file within two years of the first collection activity of the IRS (although this has not held up in tax court).

4. No assets were transferred between spouses as part of a fraudulent scheme.

5. The husband did not transfer disqualified assets to you, as defined in code 6015(c)(4) (b).

6. You did not have any fraudulent intent when filing, or not filing, the return.

7. The liability from which you are requesting relief is not from an item on the return that is yours.

IN ADDITION, THE FOLLOWING MUST BE TRUE:

1. You are divorced or legally separated from the other tax return signing party or have lived apart from the other party for the preceding twelve months.

2. On the date you signed the return, you had no knowledge or reason to know that your spouse would not pay the tax liability. You must establish that it was reasonable to believe that he would pay the tax liability.

3. You will suffer an economic hardship if you don't get the relief you seek.

The IRS will consider all facts and circumstances and not just a single factor. It is critical that you develop your arguments under each category.

INNOCENT SPOUSE CASES ARE BEST SUITED FOR PROFESSIONAL REPRESENTATION, SO PLEASE CONSIDER HIRING SOMEONE WHO HAS EXPERIENCE. CONSIDER BORROWING THE MONEY TO PAY THE FEES IF NECESSARY.

If you cannot hire a professional and must proceed on your own, consider buying a professional guide on preparing innocent spouse relief cases. Sometimes you need to have a more in-depth technical manual.

Just remember, as with any collection case, assuming you waited till this reached the collection division, you must appease the collection officer. Make sure you get an agreement (verbal is OK) to stop collection action during the time you are preparing your relief request. Once you have prepared and given it to the collection employee of the IRS, make sure they agree to stop collection action during the process.

If the IRS employee refuses the request, she will want your financial statement information, Form 433A, and possibly 433B and the required backup. You can do this if you want, or you could complain to the group manager that they should wait.

Mention that you will be seeking the opinion of the Taxpayer Advocate, and the IRS employee may back off. If not, ask for the phone number of the local office, or look it up, and tell the office that the collection division refuses to hold off collections while the IRS looks into your valid claim of innocent spouse.

Remember to prove hardship, and let them know that the collection person wanted financial statements and backup. You need to be truthful with any group managers and the Taxpayer Advocate's office about the collection officer's position as well as yours. If you make the argument one-sided and don't give equal weight to the collection person's side of the story, your credibility will be weakened.

On the other hand, if you do give equal weight, you will be seen as credible and may sometimes be believed over the collection person. State your disagreement and your feelings as if you were talking to an impartial mediator. The IRS is not your enemy.

Use Form 8857 Request for Innocent Spouse Relief to apply. Also complete Form 12510 Questionnaire for requesting spouse. The form is filed with the RO assigned to your case or with the Appeals officer if you are in an appeal.

Most people don't address this issue until it hits collections, but if you are really serious, you see that this liability is coming from an audit, and you receive a 90-day notice of deficiency, then you could also file a tax court petition within the 90 days to preserve your rights. This way if you lose, you can go to tax court. You will need to hire someone to represent you, though.

If you were to wait till a collections officer contacted you, he would normally back off, giving you a chance to file and resolve this claim. If not, you could file a CDP appeal. If there has been an abuse situation, put the following on the top of Form 8857: "Potential Domestic Abuse." Then explain the abuse in a separate attached statement.

CORRESPONDENCE YOU CAN EXPECT:

1. A letter acknowledging receipt of the Innocent Spouse claim

2. A letter notifying the non-requesting spouse of the preliminary decision to grant the relief

3. A questionnaire for the non-requesting spouse

4. Preliminary letter granting the relief

5. Letter notifying requesting spouse of final approval of relief

6. Preliminary letter denying relief and giving you appeal rights

7. Notice advising that the requesting spouse is not entitled to relief and the right to tax court

8. Letter to taxpayer with a discussion about the relief

The forms and questionnaires are self-explanatory once you are clear on what code section you qualify under. After you do your research on your qualifying arguments, fill out the form to reflect the "picture you are painting" of the situation. As you know, you should never contact the IRS by phone or by sending in forms unless you have prepared your picture that you are presenting of your information and situation.

It's OK to call the IRS to try to get information while you are getting your information together. You must be willing to hang up if asked questions beyond the initial identifying ones; avoid answering additional questions.

THE TRUTH AND LIES
ABOUT BEING AUDITED

AUDITS ARE SELECTED BASED ON IRS PROGRAMS

One program looks for compliance, and another tries to find errors. The IRS has not examined your return yet. Are you afraid? These days, auditors tend to be nicer. They tend to be more educated than the collection officers.

Of course, you have to say things like "I forgot," or "I guess I made an error," or "I can't find the proof for the deduction." You can't say, "Oh yeah, my friend the accountant said I should put down a lot of expenses because there is less than 1% chance of being audited."

There may actually be less than 1% chance that you will be audited, but you have to be careful not to say you 'willfully' did anything you know was wrong in the preparation of the tax return. If you follow this manual, you will have very little to fear—unless, of course, you can't document the items on your return and don't want to deal with the increased tax liability.

THE TWO TYPES OF AUDITS

These two types are correspondence and face-to-face. If either produces a tax liability, then the IRS sends you an examination report. You have 30 days to appeal it. In a face-to-face audit, the letter will ask you to provide information to back up certain items on your return, so you should prepare two sets of proof: one directly responding to the letter and another proving all the other items on your return.

Be mindful of things such as depreciation, loss carryovers, and so forth that affect other years. Make sure that you are prepared to defend all deductions, including carryovers to other years under audit. Purchase an audit guide from the bookstore to supplement this information, if you wish.

Explaining the business purpose entails knowing the tax law pertaining to the deduction, so take the time to look it up. If you can't convince the auditor, obtain a list of what would be acceptable proof, and have it by the due date the auditor gives you. Remember: Do not assume that it was received on time. If mailing, copy everything and send it certified return receipt.

Call the auditor to make sure that it was received on time. Or you may have hired a representative to help you from this point. You always have the right to hire a representative at any point in any IRS matter! Don't ever forget that.

It is not necessary, or better, for the taxpayer to sit face to face with an auditor to prove income and expenses. You should not let the auditor into your home or office to conduct the audit.

If you are representing yourself, set up the audit at the IRS office, or get the auditor to agree that you will promptly mail the information, requesting that it be handled that way. Tell the auditor you will put the request in writing along with a signed notarized affidavit so the manager can accept or deny the request. If your request is denied, then meet with them. This is not a battle to fight. Winning it doesn't directly reduce your liability, so save the battles for when it counts.

As in all dealings with the IRS, whether collections or audit, never adopt a guilty posture - or any posture, for that matter. Treat the audit as a routine examination of documents, and explain the business purpose.

Remember that the auditor has no collection power and can't do anything against you other than make up an examination report against you. So don't be intimidated; be nice and cooperative.

Never admit to any wrongdoing, even if you have a good excuse. You do not want the auditor to document that you willfully left out income or put down expenses that you did not incur. This is the beginning stage of fraud and criminal cases against taxpayers.

It is really OK to say that you forgot, don't remember, or don't have a reason or doing something. Maintain your innocence! Be persistent in your response no matter how much the auditor may push you for reasons.

Always pull the third-party payer information or get it from the auditor ahead of time. If there is incorrect W-2, 1099, or K-1 information filed against you, it's best to resolve this prior to the audit.

If at any time during the audit you feel uncomfortable, just get up and say that you don't feel well. Tell them that you will call later or the next day to reschedule. Do this if you need time to think. If you decided that you want representation, inform the auditor and reschedule the appointment. Request a rescheduling if you need time to obtain additional proof when your current proof is not accepted. You are entitled to this.

You can make a request to record the audit if you do so at least 10 days prior to the audit. If you start out not trusting the auditor, he won't trust you and will be more hardnosed about your proof. If you start quoting IRS publications and taxpayer rights that may not go over well, and you may get an examination report that gives you no choice but to go to Appeals to have your proof reviewed properly.

When gathering your proof, if you don't have a mileage log for your business miles, create one. Don't try to make it look like you did it during the year being audited. You are allowed to create it now for the year under audit. If you are missing receipts or need to swear to a condition or circumstance that makes an expense deductible, prepare an affidavit swearing that you actually spent the money, and tell what the reason was.

Use an affidavit to swear what your income is in cases where the auditor wants to add income but doesn't have a third-party payer (W-2 or 1099 etc.) to back it up. If the auditor has third-party payer information to back it up but the information is not yours or is higher than you actually received, you need to prove that it is not your income.

Go to the issuer to resolve it by having them issue a correct one, or do an analysis of your income and expenses to show that you didn't receive that money, if you can. Now you see why it is important to obtain the third-party payer information first. Remember, when doing an affidavit; give a lot of detailed, simple, logical explanations that will clearly lead anyone to your conclusions. Leave no room for doubt.

If you disagree with the examination report from the auditor, get your documentation together and discuss it with the auditor again. If you remain unsatisfied, seek the manager's opinion. If the issue is still not resolved, you can go to the Taxpayer Advocate and prove what a hardship it would be if you suffered a large tax burden, or unfair one, from income caused by disallowing expenses of which you have proof.

Don't forget to file an audit appeal before the due date, even if things seem to be going well with the manager or Taxpayer Advocate. They may not resolve your issues in a timely enough manner for you to be able to appeal it, so the audit appeal extends your time to challenge it at Appeals.

You may avoid an audit by explaining any items that would be a red flag. If any deductions look too large to you in relation to your income, just attach your evidence as part of the tax return. Even if the IRS disagrees with your proof and wants to disallow the expense, they probably will not charge the negligence or substantial understatement penalty.

They really shouldn't charge any penalties, but fighting the late payment penalty may entail more time and trouble than it's worth. Make sure your evidence is very specific and detailed, just as is required in an affidavit. Show that your deductions and positions have a reasonable basis in law and in fact.

Do you still feel that you are up to representing yourself in an audit? If not, call us at (800) 838-6665 or email us at info@tax-help.com before it's too late.

DO YOU FEAR THE IRS?

The IRS relies on taxpayers being scared of the consequences of not filing or paying their taxes. They prey on that fear to effectively get people to file and pay not only their taxes but also high amounts of interest and penalties.

Scared of an IRS seizure? Although many IRS representatives will try to get your business by telling you that the IRS will seize your house, car, bank account, wages, land, and so on, the truth is that seizures don't happen that often. If you make the effort to file any delinquent returns and to negotiate any taxes owed, the IRS won't try to seize your property.

DEFINITELY DON'T FEAR THE IRS

Educated taxpayers with experienced representatives know they have ways to avoid becoming a victim of the IRS. The IRS only has as much power as people allow it to have. Unfortunately, we are often so scared (waiting until the last minute to get help) that we allow ourselves to be frightened by unprofessional tax representatives. Do not become a victim of IRS collection procedures.

Call us now at (800) 838-6665 or email us at info@tax-help.com for additional questions or assistance.